T0026158

THE HARD WAY OUT

THE HARD

WAY OUT

My Life with the Hells Angels
and Why I Turned Against Them

**Dave Atwell
with Jerry Langton**

HarperCollinsPublishersLtd

The Hard Way Out
Copyright © 2017 by Dave Atwell and Jerry Langton.
All rights reserved.

Published by HarperCollins Publishers Ltd

First published by HarperCollins Publishers Ltd in a hardcover edition: 2017
This trade paperback edition: 2018

No part of this book may be used or reproduced in any manner whatsoever
without the prior written permission of the publisher, except in the case
of brief quotations embodied in reviews.

Some names and details in *The Hard Way Out* have been changed.

HarperCollins books may be purchased for educational, business, or sales
promotional use through our Special Markets Department.

HarperCollins Publishers Ltd
2 Bloor Street East, 20th Floor
Toronto, Ontario, Canada
M4W 1A8

www.harpercollins.ca

Library and Archives Canada Cataloguing in Publication
information is available upon request.

ISBN 978-1-44345-039-3

Printed and bound in the United States

HB 10.20.2023

Us—Dave Atwell

For the wife and kiddies, who did you expect?

—Jerry Langton

CONTENTS

1. A Day in the Life of a Hells Angel   1

2. Straight Outta Suburbia   14

3. Putting My Skills to Work   30

4. Playing Above My Weight Class   48

5. The Two Dave Atwells   69

6. Playing in the Big Leagues   93

7. The Big Change   111

8. The Royal Treatment   129

9. Full Patch   143

10. Behind Bars   173

11. A New Plan   187

12. Back in the Life   209

13. Undercover   220

14. The Danger Zone   232

15. Out of My Hands   250

Acknowledgments   263

1

A DAY IN THE LIFE
OF A HELLS ANGEL

Back in 2002, I'm pretty sure that my workday was not a lot like yours.

Believe it or not, like most people, my day started at around 7 a.m. I was always an early riser, and I'd wake up at about the same time even if I'd been up for three or four days straight.

As soon as I was ready, I'd head out to meet the boys. But first, I'd stop at a little hole-in-the-wall place called the Fish Joy. Sandwiched between a dentist's office and a Chinese restaurant in a nondescript little strip mall at the corner of Brimley Road and Brimorton Drive in Scarborough, it was a fish and chips place, but I generally went there for the all-day breakfast, and because I knew it well.

I was a Scarborough guy, and that actually meant something to us back then. If you're not familiar with it, Scarborough is a huge community of more than half a million people just to the east of Toronto. It's officially part of the city of Toronto now, but it wasn't when we were growing up, and it still feels different. People in what we call downtown, the proper old city of Toronto, dis Scarborough all the time, calling it "Scarberia" (because they say it's isolated and without culture) or "Scarlem" (because of its prominent black population and reputation for crime), but we never saw it that way.

When we were young, Scarborough was exactly where we wanted it to be—a real-life embodiment of the Canadian dream. We were all middle-class affluent and had nice big houses with yards and garages. The streets were wide and safe. We knew everyone in the neighborhood. We were those kids who played road hockey and shouted, "Car!" and dragged the net out of the way when someone wanted to get through. We went down to the creek to fish and later, as we got older, to enjoy a few ill-gotten beers. It was, to our way of thinking, exactly how people were supposed to live.

So I felt totally comfortable and at ease in a place like the Fish Joy. It was small, and not much to look at inside. At the back, just in front of the kitchen, there was a counter where you could place your order. And in front, between the beige, mostly artless walls, were four cheap Formica tables (three four-seaters and one two-seater) with throwaway bended steel and gray vinyl chairs. The whole place smelled like french fry oil, which always made me a bit hungrier. But I wasn't dining at the Ritz; I was just getting a solid breakfast and maybe a few early beers in a place I grew up in.

I was generally the only person who sat down there. Most people went to the Fish Joy for take-out, and many who had intended to stay and eat quickly changed their minds once they saw me. I should explain here that I'm a big boy—at least I was back then. I'm tall, about six foot, and for much of my life I weighed more than three hundred pounds. And I was a biker. Not just a biker, but a bona fide hardcore Hells Angel full patch. In fact, I was sergeant-at-arms for the Toronto Downtown chapter. And I looked like it. I'd come in wearing jeans and a T-shirt with heavy leather boots and a prominent, but totally legal, knife. Oh yeah, and I rocked a mullet back then. Even people who didn't know me knew not to mess with me.

From Fish Joy, it was a short drive or ride west to the "office." Located at the corner of Kennedy Road and Shropshire Drive in the heart of Scarborough's Dorset Park neighborhood, a bar called Country BeBop's was our meeting place. We never did any business in the clubhouse, which was farther downtown, on Eastern Avenue, because we knew that anybody could be listening there. And if the wrong people overheard the wrong thing, we could lose the clubhouse. Instead, we did it in a place we knew was ours alone.

Later, after everything went down, the media would invariably call BeBop's "seedy," but that's just lazy writing, a placeholder adjective that stands for any place you wouldn't want to bring your grandmother for brunch. BeBop's was much more than just seedy; it was nasty, like there was a flashing neon sign out front exclaiming "Crime Happens Here."

By eleven every morning, the place and the lot out front were crawling with bikers, their women, prospects, hangarounds, friends and business associates—my people. Their presence, as well as the Mad Max–like assortment of customized Harley-Davidsons and hot rods out front, kept anybody who didn't belong inside at arm's length.

There wasn't much to it. There was a meager patio tucked into the corner out front, a small bar and a tiny little kitchen. The bathrooms were downstairs with the office and a large storage area, and the main floor had ten or twelve round tables with crappy little chairs and, much to everyone's annoyance, an uneven pool table.

There was no ATM inside Country BeBop's. We all knew that having one would draw too much unwanted attention from outside because every withdrawal would be for the same amount—$40. That's because pretty much everybody who frequented BeBop's knew that $40 would get you a half-gram of coke, a Percocet and a beer. And that's all the people there really wanted.

It was a great setup, really. The bar's owners didn't deal, and could deny any knowledge of dealing going on within its premises, and the dealers had a safe place to do business, complete with an early warning system in case the cops decided to drop by.

That's what it was all about for the people who came inside BeBop's, just their daily routine, chasing their dreams one hit at a time. Other people, those whose lives have never come into close contact with organized crime or the drug trade, would never believe how mundane it all was for us. It was, for better or worse, our normal.

Billy Campbell—who we called Bald Billy—sold coke. But he was nothing like what people think of when they think of a coke dealer. He was just a guy, a truly nice guy (and his wife was a doll), who sat at a table with a log book and a bottle of Blue. He'd dole out coke, note it in his logbook, take cash, then down a swallow of beer. He'd be in by eleven every morning and out by four, just another day at the office. Except, of course, he made a shitload of cash and he'd be drunk when he left. Not stumbling, but definitely loaded. He and I had a very cordial relationship until one day, out of the blue, he told me that my girlfriend owed him $300.

If those milling around outside were my people, those who ran the inside were my inner circle. The Hells Angels Toronto Downtown chapter included my friends TC, Bully, Doug Hoyle and Bobby P.

We were all Scarborough boys who rode, partied and did business together, and BeBop's was our headquarters. We all felt safe in there. The people outside would ward off any undesirables, and warn us in plenty of time if the Doughnut Gang showed up.

Even though they were my friends, business associates and sworn "brothers," they're the kind of people who wear on you the longer you're exposed to them. So I numbed that exposure by starting my business day with a not-so-little hit of brain juice. My typical dose came in the form of a couple of big glasses of vodka—straight—with a wedge of lime.

And, usually, I'd get it from Sheila (her last name isn't important). It wasn't hard to like Sheila at all. She wasn't what you'd picture a bartender in a biker bar to be like. She had a smile for everyone who asked for a drink. She was about as tall as me, curvy with a pretty face, short, dark, curly hair. She was always well dressed and well groomed. She wasn't skanky in the least, just a good old East Coast gal, hardworking, honest and plainspoken. She was friendly and loyal, and I can still recall several times we had late-night heart-to-heart conversations and solved all of the world's problems over a few lines of coke. The thing about Sheila, for me at least, was that she was such an undeniably respectable person that it made the life we had, dealing drugs and selling stolen goods, seem normal even though we all knew society called it wrong and we could easily find ourselves behind bars for doing it.

Bartending didn't bring in a lot of money, certainly not the kind a coke user like Sheila needed, so she spent her days doing odd jobs like cleaning houses and mounting drywall. At the time, she was dating another Hells Angel, Bobby P from the Toronto East chapter. Over the years I knew her, Sheila had one other boyfriend, who I also knew. And both of them were as good to her as she was to them. They weren't the problem—TC was. She worked for him, running drugs, and he treated her like shit, no better than a fucking pack mule. She used to run kilos of coke from Montreal's West End Gang (we knew them as the Westies) to his safe house in Scarborough, and if she was just a moment late or reported to work even a little hungover, he'd lay into her mercilessly.

He was an absolute slave driver when it came to her. Despite her other jobs, Sheila always had to find the time to clean his house and sell his drugs at the gram or half-gram level. TC even used her apartment as a safe house to store his coke, weed, hash and sometimes even cash. And, loyal to a fault as she was, she never, ever dipped into his stash or skimmed off so much as a dime of his money. She was, I think, everything you could ever want in an employee.

But TC didn't see it that way. He had a simpler, more hierarchical, maybe even brutish, mentality: She worked for him, so she had to take his shit. It was hard for me to see TC be such a bastard to Sheila, not just because I genuinely liked Sheila and knew she didn't deserve such bad treatment, but also because TC had changed from the solid guy I once knew.

He had once been an old-school biker's biker. Running with Toronto's storied Para-Dice Riders, he was a hard-drinking, hard-partying tough guy. In fact, he was my original sponsor—the guy who got me into the club. But a few things changed him over the years. When the Para-Dice Riders patched over to the Hells Angels, the whole biker thing became less about freedom, having fun and being brothers and more about moving drugs, making money and protecting our turf.

Not long after we became Hells Angels, TC needed and received a liver transplant. He came out of the hospital a changed man. He was whiny—something that he never would have tolerated earlier—and he was a bully. Much to my dismay, post-transplant TC seemed to enjoy pushing people around whenever he could, no matter if they deserved it or not.

But even worse—from the standpoint of the club, at least—he'd become a cheat. He'd make bad dope deals, double-charge guys, even those close to the club, and if they couldn't pay, he'd kick their ass (or get someone to do it for him). Fuck you, pay me.

It all changed my mind about TC, my old sponsor, and I had a hard time spending any time with him unless I had a few drinks or some coke in my system first.

By the time I got to BeBop's every day, it was usually already pretty busy. Some of the guys would do anything for a buck, except maybe get a legitimate job. On most nights, BeBop's was alive with criminal activity. A seemingly endless line of boosters (professional thieves) would present their wares—I have seen them bring in everything from Weedwackers to knockoff Harley-Davidson T-shirts—and hope that someone would want to buy them. When they did, they'd give the booster enough cash for some more crack or percs, and then sell the goods elsewhere at a vastly inflated price.

It's virtually impossible for me to overstate the greed and cockiness of TC. At one point, he was even selling used cars in the bar's parking lot. And the less the buyers knew about the cars, the better it was for him. He had a dealer's license, so he'd go to the auction and buy some junkers at about $1,000 apiece. Then he'd have a friend of his doctor them up to make them just good enough to sell. For example, if the engine or transmission was making noise, Tom told me his guy would put a little Vaseline on the troublesome parts. It wouldn't solve the problem, but it would hide it long enough to fool someone into paying $5,000 for a $1,000 vehicle. I almost hate to admit it now, but I actually bought a truck from him once. And about a month after I bought it, the engine blew. It's not like I was being a jerk and doing doughnuts with it or anything like that, just driving it a very gentle three or four miles a day. When I went to him, he didn't make a big deal about it, just got his guy to put in another engine from another piece-of-shit truck he had.

One business he had that made him a ton of money was the sale of Percocet. If you're not familiar with it, Percocet is a powerful and habit-forming painkiller that addicts will sell their mothers to get. A combination of acetaminophen and oxycodone (better known as "hillbilly heroin"), taking a single pill can provide a user with euphoria and contentment. But addiction to it can ruin lives by preventing the brain from being able to create any positive feelings without the drug. Just ask comedian Jerry Lewis, whose addiction to an earlier, almost identical painkiller, Percodan, caused him to claim that he'd lost thirteen years of his life and seriously considered suicide. It can be bad shit, but on the streets of Toronto, it's gold.

And the primary way bikers get percs is through scrip scammers. They were people who would collect prescriptions for percs and then sell the pills. The best of them was a guy named Barry, a born rounder if I ever met one. He was amazing. He'd go into a doctor's office, and with a thespian's talent that would put Leonardo DiCaprio to shame, would convince a doctor to write him a prescription for percs. Then, while the doctor was out of the room or simply not looking, Barry would steal his or her prescription pad. Then he'd go home and forge the doctor's signature. Using this method, on a good day, he could bring TC as many as three hundred Percocets. The doctors either didn't notice the pads were missing or were too embarrassed to admit they'd been fooled to notify authorities.

Sheila had been acting weird; you know, up and down. One day she'd be telling me I should get out of this world, out of the business, because I was too good for it, and the next she'd be asking me for coke when I didn't even sell coke—at least, not at BeBop's.

And that's when it all changed. I started listening to her. Maybe it was because I liked her so much, or maybe it was because I felt for her after seeing her so undeservingly abused. I just wanted to help her. That was me, the kind-hearted Hells Angel. She wanted a pound of weed and a hundred Percocets, and I knew just where to go for both.

The weed was easy. There was this guy I knew named Todd, but he was so hooked up, we all called him Little Al Capone. Only twenty years old, he had a set of legit businesses in Scarborough, as well as, from what I had heard, several other less-savory operations. I had heard his guys had just come into a great deal of weed. Word on the street was that this guy named Wolf who had a huge grow op north of the city had been stupid enough to answer his door when two guys with a pizza box showed up, even though he hadn't ordered any pizza. Rookie mistake. The guys muscled their way in and made him stand on a table while they stole all his dope and cash. At the same time, some friends of Todd's let it be known that they had a great deal of weed they wanted to get rid of.

I knew I could get some because Todd was always telling me, "Anything you want, you come to me." I also knew that he never even would have spoken to me if I didn't wear the Death's Head patch on my back. In his world, a Hells Angels patch meant I was good people. I could be trusted.

And the percs were even easier. Barry sometimes had more percs than he could easily get rid of, and he had just scored with a stolen and forged scrip. I picked up a hundred from him for $2.50 a pill, and sold them to Sheila for $4 each—sure, I liked her and wanted to help her, but I wasn't running a charity.

For about eight months, I had been seeing things that gave me the feeling I was being watched. I'd see the same cars over and over again, see the same strange faces hanging around. Doug told me not to worry about it, that, yes, it almost certainly was the police, but it was little more than a formality, just part of being a Hells Angel. The cops wanted to feel out who you were, where you fit in and what you did. I tried to convince him that it was more than that, that I had seen the same guys in different cars and different people in the same cars. He blew me off, telling me I had nothing to worry about. But what we didn't know at the time was that the Ontario Provincial Police had recently tripled both the budget and manpower of its Biker Enforcement Unit for the express purpose of eliminating the Hells Angels from the province.

There were lots of vehicles hanging around suspiciously, and there was this one blue van that really started to bother me. I saw it everywhere, often with different people behind the windshield. One day, not long after I sold the weed and percs to Sheila, I noticed the same van was hanging around BeBop's, so I decided to put my theory to the test. Wearing my full colors, I got on my bike and rode away from BeBop's. To my utter lack of surprise, the van followed. I took Lawrence Avenue to the Don Valley Parkway and rode south, getting off at Queen Street, and so did he. So I rode up to the clubhouse on Eastern, stopped, and got off the bike, but left the engine running. He parked, got out of the van and began to approach me. Now that I knew what was happening, I decided to play with this guy. So I jumped back on my bike and yelled, "You're burned!"

After that, things seemed to simmer back down to normal. April 3, 2002, seemed like an ordinary day. After doing my time at BeBop's, I'd been with a girl, made my way to my dad's house (where I had been staying), had a swim and a shower and settled down for a quiet night at home with the old man. We watched a movie and then I said good night to him before I fell asleep on the couch.

The rest seems almost surreal. You know that feeling when you're not really awake, but you can sense that something's happening? I had that early the next morning. My eyes were closed and I was probably snoring, but I had the slightest, though distinct, sense that I recall the opening and closing of several vehicle doors and the sound of boots on the ground. Suddenly, the front door was smashed in and the house was alive with shouts of "Police! Police! Police!"

You might not know this, but cops actually look forward to these moments. They get high on the adrenaline rush, and not only are they trained to expect the worst, but many of them are hoping for it. They have a lot of expensive toys at their disposal and are just itching to use them.

But I was too smart for that. I put my hands up and surrendered, as they say, without incident.

Just as I'm getting cuffed, my dad—a retired vice-president of Kruger paper, standing on the stairs wearing nothing but his underwear—yelled, "What the fuck's going on?"

"Hands up!" a cop with his weapon drawn shouted at him.

"I'm sixty-five years old," my dad replied. "This is as far up as they go." That broke the tension, and the weapons were put away as I was arrested.

Almost as soon as I was charged, I knew it was Sheila who had sold us out. It might sound odd, but I couldn't actually blame her. Lots of guys in the business have a serious—you might even say frightening—lack of empathy. To them, a snitch is a snitch and to be one—depending on the seriousness of the snitching and the nastiness of the biker involved—usually warranted a death penalty.

I didn't see it that way. I knew Sheila was desperate to get out of the game, that she wanted a life that didn't involve her slaving away every hour of her life for some abusive jerk who was getting rich while she was risking a long prison stay every day for barely enough to live on. And I can't even say she didn't try, in her own way, to warn me. Sure, turning into an undercover police agent was a drastic step, but she hadn't taken any oath of brotherhood, she just happened to get mixed up in the drug trade and, like many people, suffered for it. She could get a fresh start and a few bucks for turning us all in. The risk was great, but what did she have to look forward to if she didn't change sides?

Later, when I found out that the evidence against me consisted of a pound of weed and ninety-eight Percocets, I had to laugh. Had she taken the other two? Had I? Maybe we shared them. To be perfectly honest, I really don't remember.

STRAIGHT OUTTA SUBURBIA

There was a time when I would walk into a bar and I wouldn't have to pay a cent for my drinks. They were all paid for by other people. And, as hard as it might be to believe, sometimes the person volunteering to pay was someone I had just punched out. And it wasn't just drinks. If I wanted drugs or women (or anything, really), I didn't have to pay or even ask. It was all provided for me, it was all free. It just came to me. It was an enviable life. It was one I desperately wanted as soon as I knew it existed, and one that I had in a relatively short time and in a surprisingly easy way.

If you want to know how it all happened, why I became the person I was and the person I am today, it's probably best to start at the beginning.

As I told you earlier, I grew up in Scarborough in the 1970s, and I was a pretty normal kid. But, of course, there's nobody whose life is absolutely normal, and mine started out pretty rough—I actually had to work hard to be normal.

I was born right in the middle of downtown Toronto at St. Mike's Hospital in 1965, about a block away from where the Eaton Centre now stands. I immediately contracted a tough case of asthma, and most of my infant and toddler years were spent in and out of hospitals because of it. And since I spent so much time in hospitals and in transit during that period, I missed out on a lot of things most people find quite basic—like reading and math fundamentals—and that would come back to haunt me when I was in school.

My parents were pretty much what you'd expect from an upper-middle-class Scarborough family of the era. My dad had gone to the University of New Brunswick to study mechanical engineering, and he met my mom—a fashion designer and coordinator—in Montreal.

He was a totally easygoing kind of guy, born to be a salesman. Everyone liked him. He had that uncanny ability to make you feel like you're the most important person in the room, no matter what the situation. That's an excellent quality to have in sales, and it made him very successful. And he had a way of putting things in perspective for me. Like, whenever I compared my career path with his, he would say something along the lines of: "Look, I got lucky; I got in at the right time, in the right place; not everyone can say that. Keep doing the best you can and the chips are going to fall where they're going to fall." He would also tell me that losing isn't the worst thing; the worst thing is not getting back up and fighting. All of his lessons would stick with me for the rest of my life.

My mom, on the other hand, was totally high-strung. I couldn't do anything right in her eyes. If I got an A on a report card, she'd ask me why it wasn't an A-plus. But who I am kidding? I never got any As—never got any Bs, either. But it was always something. Before I would take off my coat when I came into the house, she would be on me about hanging it up. Before I finished eating, she'd be on me about doing the dishes. To be honest, I wouldn't have minded any of that if I actually ever threw my coat on the floor or left my dishes on the table, but I knew that was never an option in our home. It just never happened. But my mom had to pick on me about trivial matters like that all the time. Her mom, my grandmother, actually told her to lay off me. I remember her telling my mom that she should leave me alone or she was going to drive me out of the house. And she was right.

My mom was successful at her job, she was friendly with people, she was pretty and she was very high-maintenance. In fact, as I look back on her, of all of her qualities—and there were many— the one that defined her was that all-too-easily tossed-about phrase "high-maintenance."

My parents, of course, were very concerned about my health and wanted the best for me. One pediatrician recommended that they get me into sports, saying that it would help build up my lungs. He could not have been more right.

For a long time, like many other Canadian boys, I lived and breathed hockey. My dad would take me to early-morning practices all over the Greater Toronto Area. If I did well, maybe if I scored a couple of goals, he was the one cheering the loudest. And if I was dragging my ass around the rink, he would yell things like "Get the lead out!" I appreciated that. It helped me. Those were good times.

I wore my hockey jacket with outsized pride. Even at a young age, I sensed that my teammates and I were a level cooler than the other guys—we were "it" at Edgewood Public School. It was a feeling I continually tried to re-create later in life.

But my childhood wasn't all easy. I was nowhere near out of the woods with asthma yet. I still remember receiving "get well soon" cards from my classmates while I was lying in an oxygen tent, watching *Uncle Bobby* and *Mr. Dressup* on the hospital TV.

And I wasn't the only one who was sick. My mom also fell ill, and I was sent to live with my dad's parents. They were very British, and everything was totally regimented from the time I got up until the moment I went to bed. My sister went to my mom's parents, and for a year, the only time we saw each other was at Christmas.

But when our family was reconstructed, it was better than ever. We moved from the Brimley and Ellesmere area of Scarborough to West Rouge, down by the lake. It was an awesome community, very close. In fact, I looked at Facebook recently and saw that all of my old friends from all those years ago are still friends today.

I never actually had any close friends until we moved to West Rouge. But I got pretty close to a guy named Donnie in Grade 6, just after we had arrived there. He played hockey too, and our parents quickly became friends, which made it pretty awesome for us. Our dads would take us fishing on the opening day of salmon season. We would always sleep over at Donnie's house and get up early to find the best spots. Donnie's dad and mom were a great influence on me, and his brother and sister were always good to me too. Both sets of parents knew that as long as I was with Donnie or he was with me, we were both safe. Donnie and I kept up the fishing tradition until we were into our twenties. Even now, I've learned that Donnie has the same salmon fishing tradition with his sons. I really wish I could be a part of that, and I certainly miss Don. We went our separate ways, mostly due to my itch to get out into the action. He knew better.

Despite my health problems, or maybe indirectly because of them, I was a big and athletic kid from a very early age. The edge I had on most of my classmates got even bigger when I failed Grade 7. I wasn't a dumb kid; I just spent too much time fucking around with my friends instead of paying attention. I think they were trying to teach me a lesson by holding me back, but if they did, it certainly wasn't the one they intended. It mostly just made me a year older and a lot bigger than the kids around me.

Back then, I was the definitive example of a Canadian middle-school tough guy from the '70s. I wore a checkered lumberjack jacket under my hockey jacket, jeans (always Levi's), T-shirts (usually with something like Led Zeppelin on them) and Greb Kodiak boots, like all the guys did back then. I had long hair, pimples and a ridiculous three-hair mustache. And, like pretty well everyone else, I could usually be found on my ten-speed bike. Because I was really into sports, I began working out pretty early and, unlike most of the guys, I never started smoking. I couldn't even if I'd wanted to, because of my asthma.

We all listened to the same music: KISS, Led Zeppelin and Supertramp. I remember we passed around those albums so often they'd come back with the covers falling apart.

It was a great time. Our routine was pretty simple, but idyllic in its own way. Weekdays were all about school, homework and messing around. When Mom made my lunch, it was something creative, tasty and untraditional. When Dad made my lunch, it was white bread with a half inch of butter and a slice of baloney. Weekends meant hockey practice, games, fishing, visits to the Scarborough Town Centre mall and sleeping over at one another's houses. We would stay up every weekend to watch *Saturday Night Live*, and then we'd imitate the Coneheads all week at school, only to do the same thing the following weekend.

And to cap it off, my dad took us on a two-week vacation to Maine in the summer of 1978. It was the first time I had seen the ocean, and I absolutely loved it.

Most important, it was about then that the Ventolin asthma inhaler became available. It kept me out of the hospital and on the ice. Precious to me, I carried it in the pocket of my denim jacket, along with my buck knife and my house key.

But hockey was the one constant. I loved the sport, not just for the same reasons the other guys did, but because I knew it also kept me out of the hospital. That would change, though. I remember this one time, I was skating around and couldn't see because my helmet kept sliding down over my eyes. When I got off the ice, my dad told me what the problem was. We had bought the helmet when I had a big pile of hair on my head, and since I'd gotten a haircut, it didn't fit anymore.

As much as I enjoyed it, hockey would fade out of my life as I got older and bigger. It's not that I lost interest in the sport; I literally outgrew it. It wasn't that I got all that tall, just big. My shoulders were wide and my chest was big. I just wasn't shaped for hockey anymore. I went on a major growth spurt and things just didn't feel right on the ice anymore. I was totally awkward. Things that had been natural for me for so long no longer were. I went from scoring about forty goals a season to four and kept piling up penalty minutes at an alarming rate. I knew it was time for me to take off the skates.

But it was replaced by something I enjoyed even more. Although my frame was no longer suited to hockey, it was perfect for high school football. Certainly, my coaches thought so. Although I was primarily a defensive tackle, I was also on every special-teams crew and rarely left the field. And my girlfriend, the same one I had throughout high school, was a cheerleader.

One of our coaches was a guy named Tony Polaro. He was about twenty-six or twenty-seven and said he had been with the Hamilton Tiger-Cats of the Canadian Football League. He wasn't a teacher, he just showed up one day and asked if he could coach. I'm not even sure if they paid him or not. It didn't look like he needed money. He showed up every day in a Burt Reynolds–style Pontiac Trans-Am with a T-top roof (except, since Tony was a total Guido, the car was bright white instead of black).

After we all got to know him, Tony opened a bar in Pickering and told us he was looking for staff. I lied about my age—it was 1982 and I told him I was eighteen when I was really seventeen—and got a job as a doorman. He knew I was big (maybe 260 pounds), strong and tenacious and that I didn't back down from fights; and those were apparently all the qualifications I needed.

Pickering wasn't far from Scarborough, but it was very different. Tony's place—Joxx Bar & Grill—was an attempt to bring a downtown Toronto vibe to a decidedly blue-collar town. He had a sign near the entrance, like many urban establishments do, with rules that included things like no sleeveless tops, no bare feet and no hats. But it didn't go over well with the locals. Those fucking rednecks either couldn't read or understand the rules or thought they were tough enough to ignore them. That was a bad idea on their part. I got in tons of fights over hats in the bar.

But he did bring one downtown Toronto tradition to Pickering that actually worked: the lineup. We'd put some velvet ropes up outside and station a doorman with a clipboard at the entrance. A guy would pass by, see that and hear the music blaring from inside and think that the place must be jumping. You couldn't see inside because Tony had had all the windows painted or covered with blinds. There were two sets of double doors, so if a guy got curious enough to want to see inside, he'd have to come into the vestibule. That's where the doormen stood, and once the guy was that far, he was sort of obligated to go in. Invariably, the guy would pass through the second set of doors to see maybe half a dozen other guys just like him, also wondering where the party was.

At least Tony always hired hot, hot waitresses, and he would also bring in guest DJs from the city and comedians from Yuk Yuk's, so it was a pretty happening place by Pickering standards.

While it did take the locals some time to catch on, the Joxx formula certainly was a success. Not long after it started to get popular, five or six copycat establishments popped up in the same area.

For me, it was a great place. Some of the other doormen were friends of mine from the team, and so was the house DJ. If my parents came in, their drinks were on the house. And all I had to do was stop any trouble before it got out of hand. That wasn't too hard. I'm not going to say I enjoy fighting or that I ever started a fight, but I didn't mind finishing any that came my way.

It was a great place to be for a young guy like me. But it wasn't long before I realized I was playing in the minor leagues. Every once in a while, Tony would bring in doormen from some serious Toronto clubs, like the original Rock 'n' Roll Heaven, which was in the basement of the Hudson's Bay Centre at Yonge and Bloor and the Falcon's Nest on Midland Avenue, just off the 401 in Scarborough. Sometimes it would be because they had a girlfriend working there, and sometimes they'd just be there to say hi to Tony.

They didn't wait in line. You couldn't make these guys wait in line, they were that hardcore. Some had done time, and I know some were steroid dealers. And they were huge; so big that they'd just eat a guy like me without thinking twice. Those guys with their fancy cars, expensive suits and huge muscles became my idols right away. They lived a different kind of life. They showed up, and people stood in line to serve them. They never lifted a finger or spent a dime, and they'd have a triple rye on their table before their butts hit their seat cushions. There's a certain mystique, even romance, about guys like that who live above the rest of society's rules. Maybe it doesn't affect most people, but it certainly did affect me. I wanted to be one of them badly.

I'd watch them while I did my own job. And I could tell they noticed me. They took to me right away, telling me they knew I was the type of guy who'd never back down. That separated me from the rest of the high school guys who were clearly less serious about the job. And they liked the way I handled myself once a scrap got started. That all goes back to some advice my uncle Larry gave me. Larry was an old-school Montreal rounder who'd been in more fights with everyone from cops to robbers than I'll bet even he could remember. He was my mom's brother, and she tried to keep us from his influence, but it was impossible. And he taught me how to punch for a knockout. The secret is to aim for the back of the head and follow through as though your fist would exit through the chin. It works surprisingly often, and I left a lot of guys on the ground.

One time, I was talking to some of the big-time guys when one of them, Ang, started telling the others about a fight he'd seen me in. "I've never seen a guy hit a guy like Davey did," he told them. "Sent the guy right over his own Camaro." Funny thing about Ang: although the other guys treated him with respect, I never heard about him breaking the law. He's a cop now.

Anyway, before long, I had a job at the Falcon's Nest.

It was a very different place than Joxx. There were always lots of hot girls around and live bands—many of which, like Glass Tiger, later became quite famous. And there were drugs, lots of drugs, drugs everywhere—doormen sold drugs, DJs sold drugs, even bartenders sold drugs.

And it's where I really honed my abilities as a fighter. I always gave the guy a chance to defend himself. You know, I'd tell him to put up his dukes, just like in the old movies. I wasn't being altruistic. I'm a pretty good boxer, so once I saw the guy get into his stance, I could immediately assess everything about him as a fighter. I'd look at his feet and his hands and quickly determine what he knew and what he didn't know about fighting—his weaknesses would quickly become obvious to me. After that, he was done.

When I had to beat a guy down, I'd always let him know who did it to him. I'd point at something like a broken nose and say things like "Tell 'em Dave Atwell gave you that." So it wasn't long before I heard my name bounce back to me like radar. But the stories tended to grow with each telling, through no effort on my part. I'd hear stories about me fighting off a dozen guys with handguns backed up by armies of ninjas in the trees, and I would always remember the actual fights the exaggerated stories were based on. Like one time I supposedly fought off this armed and dangerous gang. But the truth was that I caught three nobodies sitting on my car, smoking dope. I punched the two closest ones and the third guy ran away. I honestly didn't mind being known as a legendary fighter. I was just amused by how quickly and wildly my legend grew.

It was at the Falcon's Nest that I mastered the more subtle aspects of being a doorman. The bar was under a restaurant called Mr. D's. By day, the Falcon's Nest looked like a dump with lousy furniture and shitty carpets, but at night, with the music blaring and the lights flashing, it was pretty awesome.

There were six of us doormen on duty on any given night, and we all had jackets with the bar's name on it. We wore them with great pride. Two guys were at the front door, collecting cover charges and checking ID. Down a flight of stairs, another guy made sure everyone complied with the mandatory coat check. Farther down, there were two more guys at the double doors that led into the club.

And, finally, there was one more inside the club making sure all the aisles and fire exits were clear.

There were lots of times when I would have to escort, sometimes drag, an offending party out of the bar, and I would sometimes be greeted in the act by the police. They'd see me and some beat-up loser and start asking questions. Hey, it was their job. One thing I learned from dealing with the Durham police when I was at Joxx was that cops are generally big, tough guys who really hate writing reports. So I worked out a little speech that was something like: "Pursuant to the Ontario Landlord's Act, I attempted to escort this trespasser out of the premises, and when he resisted, I used appropriate force to accomplish said task." I'd laugh to myself when I saw them relax. They'd say things like "Beautiful, no charges here" and move on. But every once in a while, the offenders would start mouthing off and then the cops would take them in. What they did with them, I don't know, but I never asked any questions.

The head doorman was a guy named Brian. He's a successful real estate agent now, and I don't know how happy his clients would be to find out he really used to enjoy beating up drunks in bars. He was a great guy, really smart and easygoing—we became close friends almost immediately. He even got along well with my parents. But what they didn't know was that Brian's personal philosophy was that if we were going to be bad, it would be a waste of time to be half bad—we had to be full-on bad if it was going to be worthwhile.

I remember one particular night at the Falcon's Nest when there had been a surprising number of fights, and—as usual—the doormen were having no problem taking out the trash. After I had to knock out one really messed-up guy who came at me a couple of times, I saw Brian fighting a guy who didn't come out looking too good or feeling too good. And another doorman, John, eventually knocked that same guy out.

It must've been a full moon that night, because it seemed like a new scrap would start up before the last one had finished. Of course, the cops kept getting called pretty frequently, and every time they showed up, it was the same thing. The guys we tossed out were misbehaving on private property, causing damage and refusing to leave, so the cops had nothing on us; we just chalked our efforts up to self-defense and protecting the property. Back then, if you stuck to that story, you had no problem with cops.

But the cops were never at the root of any problems we had with the law. Every so often, one of the guys who got very embarrassed in front of his friends—or worse yet, his girlfriend—would try to fight back, invariably lose, and then try to get back at us. Those assholes would lay private charges or make prank phone calls, threatening to sue.

One time, at about four in the morning, my father woke me up and said Brian was on the phone, telling him someone who had been punched that night at the Falcon's Nest had died. My heart sank, of course, but I leaned on my personal philosophy at the time: It is what it is and I am who I am. Brian said he thought the guy who died might have been the guy I scrapped with, but wasn't sure.

The only thing my dad could say was, "Well, I guess we better get a lawyer."

It wasn't true. We later learned that some guy Brian "removed" had found out his parents' phone number and called them, claiming to be a police officer. He told them that Brian had killed a guy. That set off a chain reaction in which Brian, his parents, his girlfriend, Grace, my dad and I were all seriously freaking out.

But it came to nothing, like all the rest. There were a number of frivolous lawsuits against the Falcon's Nest—all from idiots who just couldn't accept the consequences of their own drunken behavior.

We never really drank while the bar was open. We had to keep our wits about us. It was only after closing time, when only the staff and invited guests were in the bar, that we began to party. And that could last all night, and then some.

Brian just got into everything in such a big way, especially partying after hours. Once, it was Halloween, so Brian and the guys stayed up all night to transform the bar into a ghost town. When the after-closing party rolled around, the Para-Dice Riders—probably the best-known biker club in Toronto at the time—showed up en masse.

I met some of them and hit it off with them right away. Some of them I liked; they were a lot like me—similar backgrounds, similar senses of humor and similar outlooks on life. Some of them I knew I wouldn't get along with. And when somebody yelled, "You want to come back to the clubhouse?" my immediate response was, "Fuck, yeah."

We pulled up to the clubhouse at 498 Eastern Avenue in Toronto's downtown Leslieville neighborhood. It's gotten pretty trendy these days, but it certainly wasn't back then. There were a lot of warehouses and car repair shops, and not much else. I thought it was pretty funny that there were a couple of police cars parked outside, like they were there all the time, just watching and waiting.

When we all got to the door, there was a problem. One of the guys we had with us, Sean, was black. We didn't know that would be a big deal with the bikers, but it was. Sean, who was from the Caribbean, was a great guy, an old friend. And he was super handsome, so my mom really liked him a lot. But that wasn't helping him here. They weren't letting him in. Before too long, though, Tom "TC" Craig, who was in charge, said, "This guy's not a nigger, he's my friend." And the guy at the door responded, "Not a nigger, eh? Must be a Paki." Sean came in and partied with the rest of us. He was welcome because Tom said he was his friend. It was just another one of those tickets to privilege, like big muscles or a patch on your back. The only problem was that the nickname "Paki Sean" stuck, and he was called that for years.

The clubhouse itself was intimidating. There were decorative planters outside that I was later told were concrete pilings that went three feet into the ground to prevent anyone from smashing a truck into the building. Every window was covered in a steel cage to prevent any projectile damage. There was a high fence with a sliding electric gate, and a lawn with a picnic table that smelled of cigarettes, weed and stale booze.

The main door was heavy and made of solid steel. Another steel door behind it slid open, only from the inside. There was always a member, prospect or hangaround in the clubhouse, manning the door 24/7. The Para-Dice Riders were very strict about the door. It could only be touched by a member—if you wanted out for any reason, you had to ask their permission or you weren't going anywhere.

The main floor of the two-story brick building was for biker use only. It had a TV, a bar, an office with leather couches, bunk beds and cupboards full of food. I would also learn that there was something of a command center in which a member could watch the feeds from several surveillance cameras set up around the building. Upstairs, there was a party room with a pool table and a long bar. The walls were covered with photographs of club members. And there was a back door that led to a balcony that was generally used only for throwing up or pissing over the side. There was only one bathroom. It was very clean, with two stalls and a couple of urinals. And nobody ever seemed to mind who was coming or going or what was happening in there.

We partied all night, and I started to think these guys were pretty cool. They had a nice setup, and seemed like they were genuinely all there for one another. It wasn't like I was clamoring over them, trying to sign up to be their newest recruit. It was more like I felt relieved and encouraged because they had shown that they were the kind of guys I had hoped they'd be—guys who would not just party together, but would stand up for one another. They were okay in my book, and I knew I would be seeing more of them.

When I was a little kid, a group of bikers went by our car. I was immediately fascinated by their loud pipes and their rebellious appearance. My mom told me to not even look at them, because they were bad men. But of course I looked, and was fascinated. I thought they were pretty damn cool.

3

PUTTING MY SKILLS TO WORK

While being a doorman was great, even then I knew it wasn't a career that would take me places or last into old age. I knew I wasn't going to go to college or university; it just wasn't in the cards. The only other thing I knew for sure was that I had no idea what I wanted to do after I got out of high school. But I did basically fall into a rewarding career that matched my skills and personality. It was one that I sincerely enjoyed, and was undeniably talented at. It's something that I probably should have kept doing, rather than getting mixed up with the things that happened later on. I can't change the past, but at least I can tell you what happened.

Just like my doorman career, the next big stage of my life started in high school. A friend of mine named Craig Bridgeman— who later became a cop—had a job with Intercon Security. He told me he really enjoyed it, said I would be good at it and recommended that I give it a try, so I applied. I liked the idea right away; not only did it pay $4 an hour (decent money for a teenager back then), but it was also an opportunity to make a career out of doing things I already knew I was good at.

When the interview rolled around, I showed up in a suit and tie—I was later surprised to learn that most other applicants didn't—and crutches because I was still nursing a football injury. When I first arrived at the Rothmans Building at Don Mills and York Mills Roads, I was seated at a table with a number of glossy brochures that described some of Intercon's services, including executive protection and mobile patrols. One in particular caught my eye. It was for their Special Assignment Group, which was a small group of employees who were licensed both as private investigators and armed guards. I could tell they were cool—they carried beepers.

I was nervous and excited at the interview, but I think I made a good impression. The suit helped, and so did the injury, I think. These guys make their living sizing up people and situations, and in me they had a big, tough kid with decent marks and a great work ethic. That goes back at least to my great-grandfather, who worked three jobs at once just to make things comfortable for his family. My grandfather and dad were the same way.

I knew a few guys from my school who had applied and not been hired, so I was delighted when they told me I was invited to their mandatory three-day training course beginning on October 10, 1983, when I was eighteen. I was hired at the lowest level for part-time work, but I was still determined to show them what I could do.

My dad was not happy about me taking a job that could likely evolve into a career that would find me bypassing higher education, but he drove me to and from the training sessions anyway. Against his better judgment, he began to get enthusiastic about the job, especially after he found out about the salaries and benefits full-time employees received. I found out later that the company's founders were profoundly opposed to the idea of unions, so they made sure to offer better-than-competitive salaries and benefits.

The course began with an introduction to the company's philosophies and hierarchy and the protocol for the voluminous amounts of paperwork that were a big part of the job. Then they moved on to how to patrol and how to spot and take care of any of a variety of potential problems we were likely to face.

Of course, it was also a feeling-out period. They were scouting us to see if we had the potential to protect important executives or if we would max out at watching a warehouse overnight.

I was nervous but patient. Every once in a while, four or five big, well-muscled guys in suits would come in and look at the trainees. Because of my history in school, I was pretty sure they were there to yank me out of class for a prank I had pulled or some comment I'd made. Instead, they were checking me out because I was actually making a good impression on them.

The instructor, who had a thick British accent, was very good, and he taught to the level of the class. At one point, he looked around the room and asked who the aspiring cop was. I had no idea he meant me. I was the only teenager in the room. The rest were older guys with plenty of life and work experience. Finally, he walked right up to me, looked me in the eye and said, "You are."

He was the kind of man who commanded respect, and so I answered as politely as I could, "Well, yeah." Later on, I realized he was the kind of guy I was willing to follow to the ends of the earth.

After I was hired, I'd hear the same thing from them over and over again about how surprised they were that some kid making $4 an hour actually gave a shit about his job.

I really did care. The idea of keeping someone safe appealed to me on a deep level. For whatever reason, the concept of keeping an individual or small group like a family protected meant much more to me than keeping the mostly anonymous community at large safe. So when my friend Craig, who had gotten me started in security, started making noises about us both becoming cops, I wasn't at all interested.

Besides, TV and movies aside, cops are rarely cool. Instead, I had my eyes on the security guys who'd made it. I mean the guys who wore dark suits, drove company cars and made $25,000 a year (hey, it was a lot of money back then) with benefits.

And it didn't take me long to become one of them.

But my first assignment was later that month. I was to patrol a new housing development in Pickering called Bayshore Cove Estates. At the earliest stages of my career in security, I had to wear a uniform, which I hated—a blazer in an odd shade of blue, gray slacks, blue clip-on tie and some stupid rubber bumper shoes. But because this was a construction site, I wore work boots (instead of the company shoes) and a hard hat.

When I arrived, there wasn't much to guard. It was basically just a big mudhole, with nobody around. I walked around the site for twenty minutes, looking for the person I was supposed to report to, panicking more the later I became. Eventually, I encountered a very pretty, well-turned-out woman in her thirties. She was a real estate agent attached to the project, and she was very helpful. She pointed me to a trailer and told me she believed there was a key hanging on a hook just beside the door. I thanked her, embarrassed that I was fucking up my potential career right from the start.

It was where she said it was, and inside I had a little security station. The first thing I did was call the Intercon Operations Centre to explain why I was late. At first, the woman on the other end of the line wasn't very understanding, but she soon changed her attitude and wished me a good shift. Inside were the two books I needed to perform my duties. The first was called the Standing Orders, and it was considered to be the bible for the account. It described everything we were contracted to do, and when we were supposed to do it. The other was called the Briefing Book, and it was where we filled in a synopsis of what we had done and seen, updated at fifteen-minute intervals. As monotonous as writing down that nothing happened at a remote mudhole every quarter hour was, I complied. I'd go and patrol the site with my flashlight, but it was in a pretty good part of Pickering, so the threat level was very low. Still, I guarded it like it was Buckingham Palace.

After a while, I saw an expensive and sporty-looking convertible pull up to the trailer. It was the real estate agent. One of the cardinal rules of Intercon was that personal visits by friends and family were forbidden while you were on the job. But she was part of the project and she was really attractive, so I let her in for a little small talk. She made a habit of stopping by, and it was only years later that I realized she probably wasn't there to talk. Had I been more experienced, I would have realized, but I was an idiot about things like that back then.

But Intercon didn't leave me all alone for my entire shift. Every night, I'd be visited by a mobile supervisor whose job it was to check up on me and to spell me for a few minutes so I could go buy a coffee or take a crap in peace.

We were told in training to always ask the supervisor, even if we knew him or her, for their company and government identification. They stressed that it was a mandatory practice. So even though I knew that when a guy shows up at the site at two in the morning in a company car, he's not there to rob me, I still asked him for his identification. He looked surprised and a little bit angry, saying, "Oh, so we're going to play that game, are we?" and taking out a tattered old card with the picture of a much younger man on it. *Shit*, I thought to myself, *I've fucked up again.* Not only was this guy a senior supervisor— who, we were told, had very little tolerance for bullshit—but he was one of the company's original employees from 1972 and a close friend of the owner.

The way he looked at my Briefing Book made me feel like I was being audited by Revenue Canada. I knew then that, even with the most by-the-book employee, he would have found something to complain about. And, sure enough, the bastard did. I later found out that he went back to the office to complain about some new kid who'd had the audacity to ask him for his identification and to brag about how he'd caught me writing down my reports every twenty minutes instead of every fifteen. So his second complaint was that I wasn't following orders diligently, and his first was that I was.

But his plan backfired. When I was confronted about his report, I told the company that I logged in every twenty minutes because I was being honest (I could have easily written down that I logged in every fifteen, something I knew many other employees did) and that the reason my reports were further apart was that I was dealing with the theft of some lumber and had to talk to the police, who came by to look around and ask me a bunch of questions.

Suddenly, my name was being bounced around the Operations Centre. They wanted more of me. I told them I'd take every shift they had. And my reputation was being enhanced in other ways as well. I once showed up with a black eye I had received from a fight at Joxx. When the operator pointed it out, I joked that it was good for the company's image. He actually agreed, and from that point forward, I never had to guard another construction site.

It wasn't long before I decided to go full-time with Intercon. I was assigned to the TD towers right in downtown Toronto. There I was, working with one of the legends of the business, Henry. He had a reputation for drinking, but I saw that one of the things that kept the account solid was his willingness to drink with the guy who hired us.

It wasn't bad, but it wasn't long before I was offered a position at the Town & Countrye Square at Yonge Street and Steeles Avenue (now Centrepoint Mall), with a chance to become a supervisor. I had to decide between shift work all the way downtown or straight days at a nearby mall full of hot young women to protect and undesirables for me to take care of. *Fuck that*, I thought. *Town & Countrye, here I come.*

I worked with a lot of people there, but some really stood out.

Nico was the director of security, a position that required him to wear a suit, and one he had acquired after years of experience and dedication. He was Italian, from a wealthy family, and, as his parents wished, he had gone to college to study to become an accountant. But he was drawn to security because of the action and excitement (nothing he'd ever experience as an accountant). We got along great, and I had no problem working my ass off for Nico.

Tony was about my age, was from the area and was a total pussy magnet. We got along great, but he soon moved to the Eaton Centre, which was where the real action was. After he left, I would frequently be approached by girls who would ask where he was and why he hadn't called in a while.

A typical day at the Town & Countrye started with checking the fire control system, the water pressure and the boiler temperature. Then we'd make sure the corridors were clear and certain doors were locked, and we'd patrol the building and the parking lot before we opened the mall. We'd make sure all the stores opened on time and that their signs and displays did not violate the common space. But the real action was always at the food court. That's where the troublemakers hung out. Every day, we'd encounter beggars, scammers, pedophiles, shoplifters, purse snatchers and a lot of gay guys cruising for anonymous sex while other people were just trying to get a bite to eat. Of course, most of the violations were petty, but the bad guys, well, they knew how to keep it interesting.

I was still working at the Falcon's Nest, and they'd razz me pretty good about being a rent-a-cop. But I knew I had a future in security.

37

I had my eye on being on the executive protection team, and I knew I had to go through some bullshit years of uniformed service, deterring minor-league criminals and weirdos in mall food courts. I had no guarantees, because I had no police or military experience, but I had faith in my unerring ability to tell when something isn't right.

But I don't mean to give you the idea that mall work is always mundane. I remember once, I was patrolling the Town & Countrye with a coworker named David when we saw a guy who definitely had something wrong with him. He just didn't look right. His eyes were all twitchy, he was sweating profusely and he was walking erratically, like he was drunk or stoned. As we both headed instinctively toward him, we received a call on our radios. They described a suspect, and every single adjective fit the guy we were intercepting perfectly. Then they told us he had just stabbed his mother forty-three times. What happened after that was a blur. We both took him down, and one of us held him (security guards were not allowed to use handcuffs back then) while the other called into dispatch, reporting we had the guy. For the life of me, I can't remember which of us did what, but I do know that both of us earned our pay that day.

All the guys went out for beers after that. Dave went to the same high school as me, but was a couple of years younger. He had an older sister in my grade who was very pretty and pleasant. I knew Dave was a good guy, really quiet, but I was really impressed by how physical he could be when he had to be. So you'd think that we would be the ones telling the story at the bar. But it wasn't us. Some guy who wasn't even there was dominating the conversation, telling all of us what he would've and could've done. So Dave and I just sat there, pounding back beers and listening to this guy's fantasy scenarios, knowing we had lived it for real.

But it wasn't all testosterone-fueled us-against-the-bad-guys showdowns. A lot of the time, the most important thing a security guard can do is to help people. While much of the job involves patrolling and making sure nobody is causing a problem or breaking into cars, we would also be the first responders to anybody who was in real trouble. The one instance I remember best, when it came to helping someone in trouble, happened when a young girl shopping with her friends suffered an epileptic seizure.

After I got the call, I headed straight for the girl, and as I was rushing to get there, I realized I had forgotten everything I had been taught about dealing with situations like this. When I got there, there was a mob around the girl. I got them to give her some room and asked if anyone had called an ambulance. Just then, all of my training on how to handle this kind of situation came flooding back to me. I took care of the girl, who was at best semi-conscious. I could have done it by the book, but I knew that seizures can rearrange clothes and allow certain bodily functions to occur, so I did my best to retain this girl's dignity (in part because she was at an age when everyone is dominated by their own self-consciousness). After the ambulance picked her up, I went back to patrolling the mall as if nothing out of the ordinary had happened. But a few days later, I got a letter from the girl's mother, thanking me for my efforts. That really made an impact.

I'm not pretending I was some kind of angel, especially when I worked with John. He was a Cape Breton boy, as tough as they come, and lots of fun. He never missed an opportunity to mix it up. Problems tend to start when the bad guys get the idea that security guards are all pussies. And those same guys also tend to believe that the cops or lawyers will bail them out for any injuries they received because of their own indiscretion. We actually had the law on our side, particularly the Trespass to Property Act and the Landlord and Tenant Act. Anyone got a little roughed up, we'd slap them with the old "failing to leave private property when directed" clause. If they dared take a shot at one of us, they were made aware of how serious assaulting an agent of the landlord really is. And when John and I worked together, Intercon's lawyers got plenty of calls. The company didn't mind. They liked the fact that we were doing the dirty work that kept the Town & Countrye safe. The only one who had a problem was that little prick of a mall manager, who would complain about John and me to Nico constantly, even though the three of us had to rescue him on a near-daily basis. I don't mind calling him a little prick, because that's what the owner of Intercon used to call him to his face, even though they were old friends and it was his first account.

I moved on, farther downtown to the Hudson's Bay Centre and then College Park, which was wild, until I was invited to join the Special Assignment Group. I was twenty-one by then, having been with the company since I was eighteen. The catch was that I had to quit my job at the Falcon's Nest. I didn't even have to think about that. I'd had some great times at the Falcon's Nest and learned a lot there, but I knew it wasn't where my future lay.

On my first night, I was to do a ride-along with a guy who'd been in the group for a while. Jim was ex–British military and didn't think much of me. He didn't say much, but he did ask me if I was former military. I told him I wasn't. Then he asked me if I'd been a cop. I told him I hadn't. Then he asked, "Then what are you doing here?" That pissed me off. How could I answer that without insulting the guy or telling him to mind his own business and still expect to learn from the guy? Still, he knew he had to do his job, and very slowly over the two 7 p.m.-to-7 a.m. shifts we spent in his car, he taught me some of the skills I would need for executive protection. I did my best to be polite and attentive and I took lots of notes.

After a few shifts shadowing other guys, I ran into Jim again. This time I had my own assignment and my own car. I was about four hours into my shift when he called me on the radio. He told me to drive over to where he was, park my car and we could talk. I was surprised to see he had a coffee for me. He told me that the only way he would be able to do his job successfully was to make sure I knew everything he did. And he became a genuine mentor and friend from then on.

I found out that he was a combat veteran. He'd seen action as a military engineer in a bomb disposal unit in the Falklands War. He'd been shot at, shot back and nearly been blown to bits.

Jim taught me techniques for discreet patrolling, surveillance, driving and alarm response. But he said the most important thing I could do was to learn as much as possible about the families we were protecting, and what threats they were or might be facing. He showed me where the clients' files were kept, and I read every single word. I was particularly interested in why they became clients and what their threats were.

Much to my dismay, they were all executives. Not a single rock star or movie star among them. But they were most of Canada's richest and most powerful people at the time.

Our job was to keep them safe, especially when they were in plain sight, so it made sense to be as discreet as possible. Every guy in the unit had the same look, one we liked to describe as "crisp." We wore conservative suits with conservative haircuts. There were no shaved heads, no facial hair and no dark sunglasses. If you had a look-at-me cowboy attitude, you wouldn't make it in our unit. Every once in a while, one of those guys would sneak in, but it didn't take long to weed them out.

When it came time to do my first daylight protection job, I was really looking forward to being able to do things other than check the house and keep an eye out for suspicious vehicles or activities. So you can imagine how crestfallen I was when my first task was to walk the client's dog. It didn't seem like security at all, just a subservient task. The dog's owner was one of the wealthiest and most influential media moguls in Canada, who also had business interests in Europe and a strong reputation in the arts community. The dog, I was told, meant the world to him, and that if anything should ever happen to it, he'd be heartbroken. *Okay*, I thought to myself, so *I'm protecting an* important *dog, at least*. Besides, I love dogs, and if someone wants to pay me to get some exercise in a park with a bunch of other dogs and their owners, I don't have a problem with that.

It was Jim who actually put it in perspective for me when I talked to him about it later. By walking the dog or performing other tasks like handling dry cleaning, I was protecting the client because I was preventing him or her from being out in the open in an unpredictable situation. Anyone could be hiding in the bushes of a public park.

Much of the job, of course, involved driving. It was our duty to ferry around the client, his or her children and their staff. The worst of these jobs was to take someone to the airport. Not only is it never enjoyable to drive someone to or from the airport, but it was also full of potential threats.

We had to know the airport inside and out. We had to know the clients' houses and offices even better. We knew if their kids played hockey or soccer and who their friends were and where they lived.

And we also got to know more about the potential threats. One prominent Toronto family had been targeted by the Irish Republican Army, so we received training in their tactics. We knew exactly how they would try to pull off a kidnapping or assassination attempt.

We were taught that there are two kinds of threats. The first is the intentional threat. This kind is perpetrated by people who study their potential victim for a long time, and who have a specific plan to harm that person. Generally, the targets of this kind of threat are high-ranking executives for whom there could be huge ransom demands if they were kidnapped. The other type of threat is called an immediate threat. These arise when the attacker has no plan and just happens upon the victim and recognizes him or her. These attacks can be just verbal assaults, but they have the potential to escalate and are very unpredictable. While those targeted by immediate threats can also be executives, especially those who frequently appear in the media, this category can also include politicians, like school board trustees, or people associated with companies that draw protesters, like furriers or certain defense contractors.

Of course, I generally got along with most of the people I had to protect. Wealthy people definitely had their idiosyncrasies, for sure, but they were generally pleasant and respectful. But not all of those I had to protect were decent people. One of my first major assignments involved Ronald Hubert Kelly. If that name doesn't ring a bell, you might know him better as Father Kelly, one of the child-molesting priests from the Mount Cashel Orphanage in Newfoundland. Back in 1979, he was found guilty of ten counts of sex abuse, involving five boys between the ages of thirteen and seventeen. It came out in court that Kelly had one of the orphans give him a blow job, and when he was done, the priest handed the poor kid a $5 bill.

Things were different back then. Probably because he was a priest, Kelly received a suspended sentence. Although he was convicted and lost his appeal, he was granted a full pardon in 1985— in other words, no actual punishment at all despite his well-established guilt for serially committing a most heinous crime.

And back then, before the internet allowed people to track them down, child-molesting priests were just shuffled off to some place where nobody knew them, or knew what they'd done, and they were often able to reoffend. Father Kelly was taken in by Archbishop Gerald Emmett Carter (he later became Cardinal Carter) of the Archdiocese of Toronto.

It was there that he started a new life. The church in Toronto put him in charge of its significant real estate holdings there. They paid to educate him in the art of wheeling and dealing real estate, and it soon became clear he had a cold eye for the best deals. Before long, he realized that he'd be better off working for himself than making money for the archdiocese, so he left the church and started operating his own business, Kelloryn (which later became RHK Capital).

And that's about the time when I met him. I'd heard some sickening stories about him, but I knew I had to put aside my own feelings and be a professional. That doesn't mean it was easy. I don't have much tolerance for that kind of thing. My own sister was once accosted at a bus stop when she was sixteen. When I found the asshole—he thought he was a tough guy, with a Fu Manchu mustache and a mullet—I beat the living shit out of him in full view of my dad and five people who just wanted to get on the bus. But this thing with Kelly was different. I had sworn to protect this man, and I would.

You wouldn't think that a dumpy little disgraced priest from a small Newfoundland fishing village would be well connected, but this guy totally was. His brother, John, was a billionaire (or close to it), and, according to the *Toronto Sun*, he was an important financial backer of Brian Tobin, who was later premier of Newfoundland and then the federal minister of industry and a guy people once talked about as a future prime minister.

Kelly really put his stamp on the Toronto real estate market with one major deal. The day it happened, we took the stretch Cadillac he'd bought from a funeral home to his meeting. I knew this appointment was important because he had on his best suit and his best toupee. I waited outside, watching him and knowing that I, too, was being watched. The deal was to buy the old Skyline Triumph Hotel on Keele Street, near the 401.

Once the deal was done, he jumped into the back of the Caddy, sat down and said, "That was a fucking home run."

Later, I remember driving to go pick him up from his home north of Toronto, when his car—a Bentley Brooklands—died on the 404 near Aurora Road. But I was prepared. Before you can drive a $350,000 car, they make you complete a course, and when things started to go bad on the 404, I remembered that my instructors at Intercon had been adamant that, no matter what happened, I was never to be stopped by the side of the road with the hood open. There was no way they wanted that image out there, even in the days before the internet. Instead, they gave us a toll-free number (this was long before roadside assistance was commonplace) and told us they'd come and take care of the problem. So I called. Forty-five minutes later, a flatbed arrived with a replacement car. I took that and they took the original back for repairs, no questions asked. When I finally got up to Ron's and explained, he just laughed and said, "My investors are gonna hate me."

Of course, they wouldn't. This guy had a knack for making them huge sums of money. But I did know that some people would really hate him if they knew more about him, so when a story came out about RHK Capital in the *Sun*, I warned him about too much publicity. "You probably don't want to be plastering your face all over," I told him. "People are only just now forgetting about Mount Cashel."

But he didn't care. He was pretty sure he was bulletproof. And he'd long since decided that money could solve any problem. For instance, there was this one kid he'd molested who tracked him down in Toronto. Not too surprisingly, the kid's life had taken a turn for the worse, and he was pretty far down the road of drug addiction. Ron's solution was to rent this guy a downtown apartment and give him a Rolex watch. Problem solved. And the longer I knew Ron, the more I realized that there were a lot of people with their hands out. But he didn't care. He and his buddies had tons of money. And a couple of bucks here and there to shut some addict up didn't really make any kind of dent in their wallets.

Kelly was hardly my only well-known client. Many wealthy Canadians have people who'd like to hurt them. One time, I was assigned to a team protecting Ken Thomson, the publishing magnate. I told him he might know my father, whose paper company, Kruger, supplied the *Globe and Mail*. He was surprised, and said that he did indeed know my father and thought the world of him. From then on, I worked for him quite steadily.

It wasn't always that pleasant. One time, my boss came up to me and said we had a job to do and that I was supposed to leave any ID at home. When I got there, I found out that some punk from western Ontario had been harassing Debbie Bassett, the young daughter of media executive Douglas Bassett. She'd done nothing wrong; this guy just thought it would be fun to mess with an innocent young girl. So we went and taught the kid a lesson. I could tell immediately he was a druggie, and so I told him that he was going to rehab. He looked kind of confused by that, so I finished by telling him that his nose was going to be so fucked up that he'd never be able to snort another line of coke. It was important to talk like that. I wasn't a psychopath, but I can tell you that it helps a lot if your opponent thinks you are. I don't believe the Bassetts asked my boss to talk to the guy, or if they even ever knew about it. Sometimes it's better that they don't know. Either way, that guy never bothered Debbie again.

4

PLAYING ABOVE MY WEIGHT CLASS

I didn't get the job, but at least they invited me to the party.

WR, my boss, had a nice, orderly home just north of Toronto. The urban sprawl had yet to roll over the area like a tsunami powered by speculation and development, so his place still had an outdoorsy, almost cottage-like, feel to it. The atmosphere of bonhomie was enhanced by the fact that members of his family, especially his very personable mother, were at the party. You can tell a lot about a guy by the way he treats his family, and WR was very kind to and involved with his. It was also abundantly clear that it was his strong family values that made WR the strong, effective and compassionate manager I had known him to be.

At first, I didn't realize the purpose for the party—WR had decided to strike out on his own. There had been a rift at Intercon once its official policy was changed so that all mobile units would share the same radio frequency. While there was some sense to that, it didn't instill much confidence in our VIP clients, because every minute detail of their private lives was being shared among twenty-five units, perhaps seventy-five people in all. Not only was it potentially embarrassing, but it was also unnecessarily dangerous. A lot of customers and employees thought it was a bad idea and tended to compare the situation to the old propaganda posters that said, "Loose lips sink ships."

Right from the start, WR was against the move. So was I. And so were many of the company's VIP clients. So when he started his own company, the Holstein Group, many of them were eager to sign with him. He broke the news to us at the party. WR explained that he had already signed contracts with many of the more prominent families who had been with Intercon and had had problems with the company's new information security policy.

Naturally, I wanted to work with him. But Holstein was way out of my league. WR was hand-selecting candidates for his new company and they were all ex-military or ex-police. He took me aside and told me the work was dangerous, and that he needed men who had proven themselves and had more life experience, pointing out that I was still just twenty-three years old. It was a stark reminder that I was just a regular Canadian kid and that I was competing with some pretty tough customers—one guy he hired had even been in the French Foreign Legion.

I didn't get the job; but, like I said, I did get to go to the party.

Although it had lost a lot of its VIP clients, Intercon was still a going concern. But a lot of the staff who had been part of the Special Assignment Group were either looking for new positions within the company or were out of a job.

John Burns, whom I had worked with at College Park, took over WR's position. Out of respect, WR had offered him a position with his new firm, but John turned him down, preferring to rebuild what was left of the Special Assignment Group, which evolved into the Protective Service Division's Corporate Resource Group under his stewardship.

John was a good guy—lean, dark-haired, and the Irish in him certainly came out when he drank. I also got along with his brothers Jim and Kevin—the latter was a cop. John had a plan for me, even though I was unaware of it at the time.

It came out in the middle of a corporate strategy meeting. The discussion was about the Eaton Centre Metrotown (now known as the Metropolis Metrotown) in Burnaby, British Columbia, just outside Vancouver. It was the new flagship mall for Cambridge Leaseholds on the West Coast, and its biggest property west of Calgary at the time. The security staff there needed a leader, and it was well known that the company was looking for someone suitable for such a big job, but nobody knew who it could be. After most of the veterans had left for WR's firm, it was anybody's guess. In the middle of the meeting, John stood up and recommended me. Since nobody laughed or sneered, I felt confident enough to apply, even though I was just a kid and had a lot less experience than most of the other guys in the room.

I got the job. It wasn't a big jump in pay, but it was far more prestigious, it gave me a much-needed change and it was also something of an adventure.

But since I had been away from mall security for a while, they assigned me to Square One in Mississauga to refresh my instincts. It was the biggest mall in Ontario, and one that, at the time, had long been plagued by gang activity and assorted weirdos. Security there is always a challenge, and anyone who's weak or timid wouldn't last a day there. Naturally, I loved it.

The chief there was a great guy named Rob Papp. He was a real man's man who loved to fish, smelled like Old Spice and really put his heart and soul into mall security. Rob was kind of flashy—he drove a white Chevy Monte Carlo SS with loud pipes—and the rest of the mall's security staff wanted to be just like him. It was, you could say, his mall.

While I was there, I was Rob's No. 2. He was running the show, and it was my job to get my hands dirty. Back then, the mall had a reputation for attracting all kinds of dirtbags, scumbags and street gangs, and I was the primary guy who stood between them and the mall's customers and staff.

When the company decided I had regained my sea legs, they wanted to fly me to Vancouver.

It wasn't that easy to leave. While the company was training me to supervise other security guards, I met a girl who worked at Ryerson University, Rachel, whom I really enjoyed hanging out with. We began spending all of our spare time together. I took her skating at Ryerson's small outdoor rink, only to find out she couldn't skate. She was fun like that, and we enjoyed our time together, whether we were sipping coffee on a moonlit patio or just hanging out. Breaking it off with her was one of the hardest things I have ever done.

Years later, I ran into her again and found that she had been keeping a scrapbook of all the times I had been mentioned in the paper or been interviewed. It was flattering and touching. In retrospect, it made me wonder why I didn't invite her to come west with me. We could have had some fun.

Leaving Rachel behind wasn't the only hard part. To be perfectly honest, we partied so hard the night before my flight that I was still a little drunk—not to mention immensely hungover—when my plane took off. Making matters worse, a friend's mom had died a few days before, and I attended the funeral before heading to the airport. When I arrived in Vancouver, the mall's general manager picked my drunk, sad, hungover ass up at the airport and drove me to my hotel. He immediately recognized my pathetic predicament and, instead of being angry, took me to the hotel bar and we had a couple of Scotches. A little hair o' the dog did the trick, and I was feeling better almost immediately.

Later that afternoon, I finally met BW. For years, the guys at Intercon had been telling me how much I reminded them of him, and some even called me "Little BW." It seemed incongruous for anyone to call me little until I met BW. We did kind of look alike, except that he was way taller and much more muscular. I mean, he was a seriously big dude. One time, when we were working out, a rep from Maple Leaf Wrestling approached BW and asked him if he wanted to be a pro wrestler. The guy had never seen him fight, didn't even know if he could; the offer was entirely based on his impressive physique. And Maple Leaf Wrestling was no joke, either. Had BW joined up, he could have been facing off against guys like Owen Hart or even André the Giant.

We totally hit it off in a way that I knew was positive and maybe even a little dangerous. When we got to talking, I found out we had actually grown up two blocks away from each other and attended the same high school. We even had old friends in common. The two of us were just a couple of old Scarborough boys with not much difference between us. It wasn't long before we were close friends, and he took me to his family home to meet his parents and sisters. We had other things in common. We'd both been through a few scares and also found that we had very similar approaches to getting shit done. Whether it was how to negotiate a bar fight or how to kill a bottle of the finest whiskey in the woods and chase it with a perfectly matched cigar, we were on exactly the same wavelength. And we both knew that our purpose in life was protecting people and property, because we knew we could.

While I was staying at the hotel, I was waiting for the valet to bring around BW's dark blue Ford Crown Victoria police special. All of a sudden, some guy—middle thirties, dressed expensively, if not tastefully, and with a big pile of blow-dried hair—pulled up in a Porsche, threw me the keys and told me his room number. Still confused, I walked into the hotel lobby and showed BW. He looked at me conspiratorially and said, "Well, that was a mistake."

Without any other discussion, we instinctively ran to the Porsche. But there was a problem. I'm a pretty big guy, but BW was a giant— at least six foot five and thick with muscle. Just getting into the tiny sports car was a major feat. Once we were in, I floored it and we took off on a wild tour of the Lower Mainland.

But then reality set in. Was this grand theft auto? I asked myself. Still, I had a buzz going from the few drinks we'd already had, I had my new best friend with me and I was driving a brand-new Porsche, so I thought, *What the hell*. We stopped at Hastings when BW saw some working girls he knew. We popped the trunk and checked out the guy's stuff. We tried on his hats, swung his clubs and even gave some of his golf balls to the girls.

Since it all happened before the days of closed-circuit TV on the streets and cameras on everyone's cell phones, it was pretty easy for us to joyride around in this guy's sports car without getting caught. Eventually, we drove back to the hotel, parked the car in the lot and left the keys on the hood. I still wonder if the guy ever got his car back. I never ran into him again.

But he did teach me a valuable lesson. As soon as I could, I got rid of the company blazer. I never wanted to be mistaken for a valet ever again.

Intercon, especially John, made the move to B.C. easy for me. They gave me a healthy relocation bonus and covered my expenses quickly and without complaint. I stayed in a series of hotels—all decent, but mostly forgettable, except for the Four Seasons— before I rented a cabin in the mountains and finally relocated to a nice apartment in Vancouver with a balcony that looked out over the mountains.

Work was pretty good. BW was the mall's operations manager and he oversaw my immediate task of training security staff that he hired. Any dummy, especially if he's big, thinks he can become a good security guard, but it's not true. What we look for in successful candidates is heart, particularly the ability to handle confrontations without backing down. That's what really matters. If someone has that, at just about any size, I can make them into a good security guard.

One of the more interesting candidates he sent me was a woman who aspired to become a professional wrestler. She and I hit it off and she used to call me while she lay naked on her balcony, drunk on tequila.

One night, BW and I were hammered and stopped by the mall for a "spot check"—we weren't working and it wasn't part of our job descriptions; in reality, we were desperate for a place to piss. When we got there, we found our would-be wrestler doing wind sprints in the mall's parking garage. Although she wasn't technically doing her job, we didn't reprimand her. Not only were we pretty clearly drunk, we were sure she was capable of doing her job and afraid she'd have us both in the old pretzel hold if we made her angry.

On another spot check, we found that one of our security guards had made a gigantic bird's nest out of shopping carts. He had been attaching them all together to get the quarters out from the locking mechanisms. His simple solution to getting every last quarter out of dozens of carts was to put the chain from one cart into the lock of another and then stack them on top of each other.

It was stupid, it was awful and it meant a lot of shit work for us, but we had to laugh at the sheer ridiculousness of the sight and how pathetic the guy who did it was. Luckily, BW had a pocketful of change and I had some quarters in the office, because if the client ever found out about it, our whole company would have been fired.

With all the young men and women working in the mall, a significant part of my job was to serve as a relationship counselor. Girls who worked retail would come to me and ask why one of my employees didn't call her. To be honest, I didn't care. But just to keep the community running smoothly, I'd talk to all parties involved, smooth things out, make it a nicer place to be.

Sometimes shit got serious. We had this one guy who would continually show up for work unshaven and unshowered; he really looked like he slept in his uniform most nights. I couldn't stand it anymore, and when he reported for work looking like some home-less creep, I really let him have it. I really laid into him—verbally, of course—and let him know what I thought of him and his attitude. Instead of straightening up and flying right, the kid called BW to complain about me. And, as unbelievable as it sounds, told him I was coming on to him. Of course, BW knew it was bullshit, but he had to treat it like any other complaint.

Not too long after that, BW, a client and I were eating dinner at a decent restaurant—not exactly the height of luxury, but certainly not a redneck dive either. I was really enjoying myself because we were drinking pretty hard, the food was good and the waitress was sexy. But after she had to go home and was replaced by an annoying assistant manager, I gave up caring and just started hammering back the booze.

The next thing I remember was waking up in my own apart-ment. I hadn't gotten around to decorating it yet. Basically, the only things inside were a sleeping bag and a tent I had pitched as a joke. Except that that morning there was also a windsurf board, one I recognized from the restaurant we were at the night before.

Although I had no memory of it, I quickly realized that I had stolen the sixteen-foot board, with its even bigger sail, from the restaurant because I was pissed at the assistant manager. I had dragged the monstrosity all the way home and somehow managed to carry it up eleven floors. Even out-of-my-mind drunk, I'm a pretty determined guy.

Of course, I was late for work that day. I had to lug the windsurf board and sail all the way back to the restaurant (which must have been easier when I was drunk because it was awful while sober). I didn't want to actually talk to the people at the restaurant, so I dropped it out front and ran away as fast as I could. That was kind of silly on my part, though. Since I had paid for dinner on a credit card, they knew exactly who I was and how to get hold of me. I'm just glad they were cool about the whole thing.

Generally, that's how it went. What happened on the West Coast was a completely different lifestyle than I had known in and around Toronto.

One of the big differences was that, because of my new position of authority, I was hanging around with lots of corporate people. While all of us guys had fun drinking, fighting and riding scooters around in our free time, at work, there was a great deal of white-collar stuff.

On the weekends, though, I would go into the mountains with BW and his wife, who was awesome. I would always bring some girl—nobody special at that point, just girls I got to know. We would take his 4x4 around the logging roads and tour some of the beautiful mountain lakes in his boat. Of course, we would also drink too much and eat too much and generally have just too much fun enjoying the fresh air in the lifestyle that British Columbia offers.

Out west, I quickly earned a reputation for working hard and playing even harder. It's not really how most people do things out there, but it had long been a family tradition that I had wanted to keep up and eventually pass down the line. There were times when I would be dropped off at work and have to furtively change in the office and quickly rinse my mouth out because I still smelled like a campfire, cigars and beer. That wouldn't cut it at most B.C. workplaces, but it was fine where I was because some of the rest of the staff had similarly hedonistic lifestyles away from the daily grind.

Before I left Toronto, my dad told me that Vancouver was a very union-oriented town. I didn't know what he meant by that, but I soon found out—the employees really do run the show there. From my vantage point as a junior manager, I saw the situation from both sides. I understood the frustration the head office staff felt, trying to enforce policies and procedures in an effort to improve the company and gain more business. But I also saw that the hardworking employees who were putting in an honest eight hours a day were not prepared to do extra work without pay so that the owners and managers could get richer. Both sides had valid points, and I was in no position to make a difference either way, so I stayed as neutral as possible and instead thought about the big picture.

Still, it could get ridiculous at times. I had one guy call in "sick" by telling me he was taking the day off because it was beautiful out and he wanted to spend it golfing. I was in a bind. I couldn't fire the guy, and I knew he wasn't going to come in under any circumstances, so I just had to let him go golfing. When I told him he could have at least told me he was sick, he replied, "You know I'd never lie to you, Dave."

I guess I was doing a pretty good job, because they offered me a choice opportunity. A coworker asked me to join him in Shanghai,

China, where he said I could become the director of the security staff for the Shanghai Center, which was a very desirable flagship account. Money was just beginning to pour into China at that point and you could see the signs of wealth sprouting up everywhere. The Shanghai Center was a state-of-the-art combination of a luxury hotel with high-dollar apartments, an office tower and a premium shopping complex with parking. With a salary of $40,000 U.S. (adjusted for inflation and exchange rate, it'd be around $100,000 Canadian now) and a free luxury apartment, it was the opportunity of a lifetime for the right guy. I just wasn't the right guy.

But I knew who was. I was working with an assistant supervisor named David West. He had a deeply instilled work ethic, even though he was a born and bred West Coast guy. I think I recall that his father was a firefighter in Burnaby. I knew without a shadow of a doubt that a guy like Dave could take this kind of opportunity and mold it into an enviable future. He was a few years younger than me, but I knew that he had a steady girlfriend and was exquisitely professional in everything he did. So when the real estate firm that offered me the position asked me if I had made a decision, I told them that I was sincerely flattered but could not take the job. I did, however, tell them that I knew a guy who would be even better suited to the opportunity.

Dave took the job and ran with it. He made a pile of money, got some invaluable life experience and found himself a beautiful wife over there. When he came back to Canada, he was a smarter and more mature person and is now doing very well in the property management game.

When I told them about the Shanghai job and how I didn't take it, my family and coworkers told me I was nuts. They said it was a perfect opportunity and I should have squeezed it for all that it was worth. But I'm not built that way. I'm not a pushover, but I'm just not at base a selfish person. Sure, the money and chance for advancement would have been good for me, but I knew that Dave would do a better job, and that he would enjoy it more. In the end, I don't regret the decision, I'm happy for Dave and his wife and I take some pleasure in knowing I did the right thing for everyone involved.

The fact that I just happened to be banging a stripper named Bandit at the time had nothing to do with it. Hell, she would have loved to come with me.

A lot of people looked down on me for that. So many guys, especially the corporate types, would sneer at me for visiting a strip joint or even going home with a waitress and taking her on a nice weekend for something like a Granville Island barbecue. I didn't see anything wrong with it; nobody's getting hurt, and everyone's having a good time. But those guys pretend they're too good, too moral for anything like that—and then they go out at night and try to do the same things behind their wives' backs. What a bunch of fucking hypocrites. Don't think that I'm talking about guys like BW. He and the others like him are solid guys who love their wives and are loyal to them. No, I'm talking about the pussies who call the shots in the security world, but couldn't walk through a dark alley without pissing their pants.

I can't say I'm proud of every little thing I did on the West Coast, but at least I was honest about everything. I never hid anything, and if any corporate guy from any industry looked down on me for hanging out at strip joints, they should remember that I saw plenty of *them* there. Fuck them.

As I was getting settled in Vancouver, an old friend from the Falcon's Nest days dropped by. I was more than happy to see her and let her stay over. Things seemed to be going great between us until one day she just freaked out. She said she was going to become a stripper and ran off.

I knew what to do. I grabbed BW and another coworker—JI, a former prison guard— and headed to the nearest strip joint. She was there, but was refusing to go onstage. The crowd was getting pretty frustrated with her act and the drunken rednecks were yelling at her to take the stage and get her damn clothes off. When we arrived, she ran to us. We quickly found a table and started having a good old time with beer flowing and conversation rolling.

That did not make the louts in the crowd very happy at all. Somehow, they got the idea that BW, JI and I were preventing her from going onstage and they began to threaten us. One of them— their self-appointed leader, I guess—got in my face and said, "Let her go onstage, it's not like you're gonna marry her."

I couldn't help it. I turned to the girl and asked, "Will you marry me?"

I knew what was coming the second she said yes. For a split second frozen in time, out of the corner of my eye, I could see in a mirror the reflection of a beer mug coming straight for my head— the fight was on.

It didn't take long for us to clear out the bar. We were all big guys who were trained in hand-to-hand combat and they were a bunch of drunken nobodies trained in nothing. My memories of it are kind of like a fight scene in a Hollywood movie. Chairs were thrown, guys were flying over the bar. The odd part was that we were in suits and ties while our opponents were in sweatpants and lumberjack shirts. And the outcome was never in doubt.

After the fight, the rednecks surprised me by asking if they could buy us beers. The bar was in no shape to serve, so we went out to the parking lot. I noticed that their pickup trucks had gun racks, so we politely finished our beers and left discreetly.

When we went back to BW's house, his wife—who was waiting up—was furious. Not only was it the middle of the night, but our faces were scratched, our knuckles were black and blue and our suits were torn and stained with redneck blood. She demanded an explanation, but the best we could do was laugh and tell her it was just another day at the office.

That only made her madder, and she reminded BW that she had a list of chores he had promised to do that weekend before he went off to have fun with me and JI. So, being a quick-thinking guy and a helpful friend, I went to the kitchen and took the list off the fridge and went immediately to work. You know you're a real friend when you're vacuuming his house in your underwear so he won't get into more trouble.

At the operations meeting on the following Monday, RP looked at us and laughed. He said he didn't want to know what happened, but that it looked like we had been in a rumble with the Hells Angels.

After the reluctant stripper went back to Toronto, there was one girl I was seeing pretty regularly in Vancouver. She was beautiful. A few years younger than me, she was a university student who was working in one of the retail stores in one of the malls I took care of. We had a lot of fun together, and she even met my parents when I brought her to my sister's wedding.

After a few years of working security at the malls in the Vancouver region, I was promoted to a sales position. I was surprised at how naturally the task came to me. I had always liked dealing with people, and that's all sales really is. Not only did I get paid more, but the company provided $900 a month for me to get a car and keep it full of gas. They even paid for travel expenses.

We were busy upgrading all of our old technology. The plan that came along with it was a smart one. We offered major technological upgrades to our customers at no cost, but would also try to upsell them on then-unheard-of devices like motion detectors and new services like door contact patrol checks. It was easier to unload that stuff than it sounds.

Have you ever met someone who—for reasons you can't quite put into words—makes you just want to punch him in the throat? BW had left the company by that time, and a new guy had come to our office. For some reason, he had a hard-on for harassing me, which was appropriate because he was an absolute dick. You know, the kind of guy who doesn't like you from the moment he lays eyes on you and does everything he can to get in your way.

We never got along, but when he offered me a severance package, it came out of the blue to me. I didn't respond to that politely. In fact, I told him I'd like to throw him out the window, but because I knew the window cleaners and knew that they had just washed the windows, I couldn't bear to make them have to do the job over again.

That didn't do much for my image at the company, so we worked out a deal and they came up with a substantial severance package. I bid sayonara to Vancouver and moved back to Toronto. Almost immediately after I arrived in southern Ontario, I started working for WR again with his new company, which by that time was thriving. And to my pleasure, it employed all the old crew, which later also included BW.

Of course, not everybody who worked there was exactly my cup of tea, but I had matured and realized I probably wasn't their favorite guy in the world either. In most cases, I decided just to meet people halfway and remember my primary purpose: keeping our clients protected. I had become a professional. Experience and a great set of teachers had transformed the young tough guy from Scarborough into something hardly recognizable.

In typical WR style, I was put to work right away. I got the midnight shift, which mostly involves patrolling and countersurveillance. That means there's very little interaction with clients, which was fine with me because the company had an almost entirely new client base, and I didn't really know any of them.

While I was away, WR had improved the conditions for his employees. The new vehicles were much nicer than the old ones, and visiting the new office was a pleasure because the environment was comfortable and the staff was enthusiastic. I tried to bring that to the table as well.

My mom and dad were nice enough to let me have my old room back until I got my feet on the ground. That took about a year and a half, in no small part because they had a swimming pool.

While it was great to be back with WR, BW and the boys, they weren't the only ones who welcomed me back to southern Ontario. My old pal Jack, from the Para-Dice Riders, was also glad to see me.

I soon started doing covert surveillance sweeps for the club while I was still working for WR's company. Because the Para-Dice Riders didn't have the kind of sophisticated equipment I needed to do the job right, I'd rent it from a guy I knew who we called Big Sean—he earned the name by being six foot ten. He was a great guy, nice as hell, and even taught me how to use the stuff.

At that point, I considered the guys in the Para-Dice Riders to be friends, but I wasn't working for them simply out of the goodness of my heart. On a good weekend, I could make $1,800 cash for a little security work. Of course, since Big Sean taught me how to use the equipment and loaned it to me with few questions asked, I felt it was appropriate to kick back a little of that revenue to him, usually in the form of beer or wings. It just seemed like the right thing to do at the time, but I would later learn that's how a lot of our economy actually works—quid pro quo with none of it on the government's books.

It wasn't just the Para-Dice Riders I worked for. Word got around, and I found myself sweeping bugs for the members of the Vagabonds and Satan's Choice. I found it funny at the time, because the Vagabonds were supposed to be rivals of the Para-Dice Riders, with whom I was pretty firmly associated by then (although they did party together). But I wasn't going to turn down good money for an easy job.

Compared to outfits like the Vagabonds and Satan's Choice, the Para-Dice Riders had some class. Their members always paid their dues and debts on time and they tended to ask intelligent questions. It was natural that they were suspicious of me, but they employed me because I came well recommended and it was clear that I knew what I was doing.

There was a world of difference between them and Satan's Choice. When I finished a job for one of their guys, I'd have to beg them for the money they owed me. It disgusted me the way their guys would constantly flash their cash, cars and jewelry but would try to squeeze every single penny when it came to paying out. They would stop at nothing to save a few bucks.

I remember one time, I was doing lines of high-quality coke with a Satan's Choice full patch who owed me money. After much cajoling, he finally agreed to pay me, but he just had to be a jerk about it. He dropped a roll of bills on the ground, clearly expecting me to dive after it. But when the roll hit the floor, it came apart and I could clearly see that it was just a wad of Canadian Tire money wrapped with a fifty and a hundred on the outside. I couldn't believe the fucking nerve of the guy.

As outraged as I was at the time, that guy later became a pretty decent friend. Funny story, he later moved in with a vegetarian girl (she wasn't vegetarian when I knew her, though) who none of the other guys approved of and who forbade him from drinking or having any fun at all. The last I heard of him was that he died of a brain aneurysm while living alone in an old van.

A few minor problems like that aside, reconnecting with both groups of guys was awesome. My schedule was set: I would work with WR's company from Monday to Friday, putting in my time there and enjoying it, and then on weekends, I would cut loose with the boys. We'd go to some club party after I'd done some sweeping work.

Eventually, my responsibilities began to expand a little, and I started doing a little collecting.

One of the more prominent Para-Dice Riders, Tom "TC" Craig, was a bartender and a doorman for one of the clubs on the Danforth strip, where he earned a reputation of being a tough, no-nonsense kind of guy. But he liked to drink, he liked to party and he liked to fight, so we naturally hit it off well right away. It soon got to the point where I would meet Tom as soon as I got off work on Friday, spend the weekend with him and then clean up real quick before going to work on Monday morning.

It was at about that time I was driving around Ronald Kelly, the disgraced priest, for WR's company. I drove him to some pretty rough meetings with some pretty bad-looking dudes. I didn't know much back then, but I knew he was dealing with some scary shit. I didn't have fuck all on me in the way of weapons, but I learned that if I looked hard and serious, the other guys would always assume that I came heavy like them.

And no one at the office was the least bit aware of what I did on my weekends because I reported directly to Kelly. Of course, I would drop into the office every once in a while to flirt with the girls and say hi to WR, maybe even crack a few inappropriate jokes, but that was it. I was doing a good job for Kelly, and that's all they were concerned about.

Every once in a while, Kelly—disgraced and vile as he was— would have dinner with His Eminence Cardinal Carter. Carter's driver, Tom, also worked for WR's company, and I knew him and was quite friendly with him. The company was something of a tight-knit family, so I would actually drive His Eminence when Tom was on holidays. Even knowing what I knew about Kelly and some of the other bad men who served the Roman Catholic Church, being trusted to drive around someone as distinguished and important as the cardinal was a huge honor for me.

It was a wild, mixed-up time. I didn't think anything was wrong with parking the car I drove Kelly around in at three o'clock on a Friday after work, meeting up with Tommy Craig, and then downing a whole bunch of beers. We'd then go see some strippers, and if one of them told us a guy owed her money, we'd track him down. And if he couldn't pay her, he'd likely get his lights punched out, maybe even get his car taken. Then we'd party all night and all day at the clubhouse. And then I'd go back to work, driving Kelly around on his nefarious rounds all week.

For me back then, that was normal.

5
THE TWO DAVE ATWELLS

It might seem like I was living two lives, but it didn't feel that way to me at the time. I was doing security at my day job, and I was doing security for the guys in the Para-Dice Riders. The big difference was that I partied with the bikers and they paid me better. All that would change, and often because of decisions made by people other than me.

By the end of 1998, things were changing at the company. WR was moving into a new direction, and some of the old-school bodyguards didn't fit into where the company was going. One of them was me. So when one of my early trainers who had returned to Intercon offered me a new position there, I jumped for it.

The job required me to provide close protection for a very well-known power company in Toronto. It was not as glamorous or fun as I was used to, but it was a lot more money. It was evening work, but it was also a steady schedule of four days on and four days off, so it allowed me a great deal of free time.

With the extra time and money, I did what a lot of guys like me do—I bought a Harley-Davidson.

At the time, I was living on Kennedy Road in Scarborough, near the 401. I was with girl who was very pretty but could be bad news. I mean, she was usually charming and fun, but she just couldn't handle her liquor. Once she had a few drinks in her, her mouth wouldn't stop. She'd be catty and taunting and really make everyone around her feel bad. Because of that, I wouldn't take her out with people very often because I didn't want to risk her offending them. Even still, she was quite popular with a number of old ladies and girls associated with the Para-Dice Riders.

So it became natural for me to start socializing even more with the guys in the club—I was already working with them and had known them to be my kind of guys for years. But something told me to stay at arm's length. Still, when Bernie "Bully" Walczak, a long-time Para-Dice Riders member, asked me why I hadn't joined the club, I couldn't come up with any reasons why.

It was the fall of 1999, but I remember it like it was yesterday. We had been enjoying some beautiful weather and we had been riding around all day and ended up, as usual, at BeBop's, where we started drinking. When I told Bernie that I might be interested in joining the Para-Dice Riders, he went over and spoke to Tommy Craig. Tommy then came over to me with a big smile on his face and said words I'll never forget: "I'd be happy to be your brother and I'd be happy to sponsor you." I knew I had a good reputation with these guys, but it surprised me how quick they were to accept me.

It was amazing how quickly the word spread. Doug Myles—who

was vice-president of the Para-Dice Riders—also stood up and said he'd be my sponsor. Even Billy Dawson, who was serving a seven-year sentence for selling cocaine, got word from behind bars that I was a solid man and said he would sponsor me when he got out.

It normally takes about two weeks for any major company's human resources department to recognize a potential employee, sort out all the necessary paperwork and establish the process for a meeting or an interview. But within twenty-four hours of Bernie Walczak asking me to join the Para-Dice Riders, I had members calling me or coming up to me in person to give me their blessing or ask me if I knew exactly what I was getting into. I was impressed by their organizational skills.

The guys in many motorcycle clubs say that they are just motorcycle enthusiasts and are involved in nothing more than a club that allows them to express their interests with like-minded individuals. They say they're not into organized crime. They say they're just a bunch of people who like riding Harley-Davidson motorcycles. And, in the beginning, I believed them—and maybe for some, it's true—so joining the Para-Dice Riders was not a huge moral decision for me. I knew some guys did some underworld-style stuff, but to me, that reflected on them, not on the club itself.

Not long after the ball started rolling, Tom Craig asked me to come over to his house. I already knew by then that Tom could be moody sometimes, and I was relieved to see he was in one of his good moods when I arrived. In fact, as I was getting off my Harley, he shook my hand and hugged me. It was a significant moment because I had seen members do that with each other all the time.

I knew that members rarely allowed non-members to touch them, let alone hug.

As soon as I got there, he made a point of telling his wife, Sharon, that "Dave is going to be a striker." Most motorcycle clubs refer to guys trying to become members as "strikers" (some spell it *strykers*) and the process as "striking." Don't ask me why. She shook her head, laughed and said, "Whatever."

Tom and I went down to his basement. He told me that they had "church" (what bikers call their club meetings) the night before and my name had come up, so it was good timing on my part to show up when I did.

And it was an auspicious time for the club as well. The Para-Dice Riders were in the process of splitting into two chapters, one called Downtown (in Toronto's Leslieville neighborhood) and one in Woodbridge, a rapidly growing suburb north of the city. I was only interested in Downtown.

Tom told me that there would be three or four other strikers going through the process with me, so I wouldn't be carrying too big of a workload. At the same time he was telling me that, he was rifling through a closet, clearly looking for something. Eventually, he pulled out a leather vest with white-and-black trim around the arms and the waist.

They were my "colors." In the biker world, your colors mean everything. They're your identification badge and your most prized possession. One of the first things strikers are told is that their colors are all-important—don't let anyone touch them, and protect them as you would your own life. They're called your colors because the color combination indicates which club you're with. We were black and white, the Hells Angels were red and white, the Bandidos were gold and red. Once someone saw your colors, he knew who you were with. I couldn't help but be reminded of how cool my friends and I felt with our hockey jackets back when we were kids.

Tommy handed me the vest and, after I put it on, gave me a hug and said, "It's gonna be a long road, but it's going to be worth it in the end, brother."

There was no going back after that. The first club function that saw me in my new black-and-white vest was a funeral for a friend of ours who was not in the club. It was for a guy named Paul, who we always called Blinks. He had taken his own life. Usually, bikers refuse to go to funerals if the deceased has committed suicide—they consider mental illness to be a sign of weakness that they will not tolerate among their friends.

But Tommy Craig, Bernie Walczak and Dougie Myles ignored the rule and attended the funeral because they cared about the guy and his family. Everybody who went arrived on their bikes, including Jack and some of the boys from the Falcon's Nest.

Even my mom had known Paul well. He was a tradesman, a very good carpenter, and she had paid him to build a deck in her backyard. She was at the funeral too. She sat with us guys. At a quiet moment before the actual service, she leaned over and asked Doug Myles, "When will David get one of those crests on the back of his vest?" She was referring to the patch on the back of the vests that only full-fledged members were allowed to wear. I was shocked. My mom was excited and hoping I'd get my full patch, like it was a college degree or something. Tommy's reply to her was, "Soon enough, Carol, but he has to be a good boy."

After the service, the boys and I laughed our heads off. We all agreed that my entry into the club was greenlit. I mean, if your mom approves, you're probably a natural. Still, my dad wasn't nuts about the idea. He wanted me to do so much more with my life.

By then, I was pretty excited about the club and couldn't wait for my first church meeting, at which I would be introduced to the whole club. It was frankly quite difficult to have to wait a whole six days after Paul's funeral. When the time arrived, I showed up on my bike and was quickly introduced to the other strikers: Jason Tuck, Tow Truck Tony, Sunny Braybrook and a guy who was just called Razor.

Sunny was a thirty-year member of the Para-Dice Riders, but he had been busted down to striker because he had invited an informant into the club and later participated with a CBC-TV news report about the incident. Tow Truck Tony was also a member who had been busted down to striker, for the indiscretion of losing a floppy disk with club information saved on it. Tuck was a young kid, but he was sponsored by Jake and Josh Neal, sons of John Neal, who was the president of the club. Razor was a friend of Steve "Tiger" Lindsay (who would later make headlines for being one of the first two bikers in Ontario to be convicted of committing crimes on behalf of a criminal organization—our chapter).

They let us know that we had to be careful. In 1997, the feds had added a new law to the Criminal Code that was aimed directly at biker clubs. Basically, if they could prove that you had committed a crime "on behalf of a criminal organization," they could give you a much stiffer penalty. And our chapter had the dubious honor of being the first to be labeled a criminal organization. Veteran bikers hated it; they called it the "guilt by association law." They felt that if they got into a bar fight, they'd get probation or just a warning, but if they got into a bar fight with their colors on, they would go to prison.

Later, in 2005, Tiger and Razor were convicted of leaning on a debtor too hard. Since they were wearing club paraphernalia, the Crown managed to convince the judge that they were using the Hells Angels' reputation as a weapon of intimidation. First, the court decided that the club was a criminal organization; then it decided that the guys were guilty of extortion "in association" with the club. That might be a legal nuance, but it sent a decidedly unsubtle message.

You'd think that would make it illegal to be a Hells Angel, but that's not how the law was written. We always thought that if they banned the Hells Angels, we would sue for our right to exist and get the law overturned. Instead, the wording of the law meant that any convictions for offenses that used the club's reputation or that would benefit the club would be subject to far stiffer penalties.

So it was made clear to us that the club was not to know about any illegal activities, the clubhouse was no place to commit crimes, and if you got caught doing something, it was your own thing, not the club's.

It was that day that I entered Stage 1 of becoming a biker. I was what law enforcement calls an associate, but the clubs themselves call a supporter. At that level, I was allowed to attend parties occasionally and to wear club support gear (things like T-shirts and hoodies with the club's logo on them). Associates have no official duties or rights, but they do enjoy a few privileges with the club and its members.

For example, if the associate is a drug dealer who is working with the member, then the member will provide the associate with protection from rip-offs and other dealers encroaching on his territory.

Interestingly, while members may only ride Harleys, associates can have any kind of bike—I saw several Hondas over the years— and nobody in the club is allowed to criticize his bike.

One less advantageous effect that occurs after a guy becomes an associate is that police start noticing him more often. If he's riding or driving, the cops will stop him to check his plates and insurance or to see if he's been drinking. No one who enters the clubhouse escapes a police probe. No one who meets a member for lunch or coffee or drops by his place to watch a game avoids a police photographer snapping a few shots for the member's official file. The police spend a lot of time and effort building a file on every member to help them determine what illegal activities he might be involved in and to have enough evidence to back up their claims in court.

Over the years, I saw a number of associates come and go. And I noticed that many of them shied away from being seen with members in public. That's due to pressure from police. Police officers will frequently visit biker associates at their places of employment. They will even inform the associate's employer of his relationship with the club and might even talk about the club's ties to organized crime. Not surprisingly, many an associate has found himself out of work as a result. So it's not uncommon for guys to keep their friendship with biker club members on the down low.

I wasn't one of those guys. I was a proud supporter of the Para-Dice Riders. I openly hung around with Bernie, Tommy, Doug and Billy. I quickly got to know Jughead, Silky, Birch and Moose. Because of the alignment between the two clubs, I was also accepted by Satan's Choice as an associate of the Para-Dice Riders. I wore support shirts for both clubs. I had a Right to Ride campaign sticker on my car. As soon as I bought my bike, Tom slapped a Right to Ride sticker on it too.

It wasn't just for show. No matter where I parked my bike overnight, even in the worst neighborhoods of Scarborough while totally unguarded, I knew it wouldn't be stolen or damaged. The mere sticker packed that kind of power and intimidation. And if members rode into a parking lot full of bikes, they would park beside mine because of the sticker. It was a visible identifier that I was with the Para-Dice Riders. I might not be a member, but I was one of their guys.

But I joined for Tom and the guys, not the club. I wasn't so much a dedicated Para-Dice Riders guy as I was loyal to my friends who were in the Para-Dice Riders. I partied with these guys, fought with them and collected money for them.

The main guy, or at least the guy who struck me as the main guy, was Tom. He and I gravitated to each other quickly. After a little while, I spent most of my days off with Tom. Sometimes we'd go fishing, and sometimes we'd go fighting. If someone looked at Tom the wrong way, it was on. He had a quick temper, and I was behind him 100 percent.

The members noticed I was always on my bike, rain or shine. That caught the attention of many Para-Dice Riders members. Donny Petersen told me he noticed me around Scarborough, riding bar to bar, having a beer here or there, with a chick on the back of the bike. He liked that I was behaving myself while representing the club. He knew that if there was a scrap, I was cool, and if everyone was laughing and telling stories, I was cool with that too.

Bernie told me that if I was serious about striking, I would have to get to know the other members well. I had already met a few of them while doing security and bug sweeps, but not the entire membership. That would come on my first run, which was to Port Dover—a beachside resort town on Lake Erie that Ontario bikers love and head out to every Friday the 13th.

Bully told me to be at the clubhouse, on my bike, early on the morning of the trip. I was there, in the fucking pouring rain, earlier than he asked me to be. Although most of the members took off on their own, I met Larry Pooler, Sunny Braybrook, Stoney and Bald Wayne outside the clubhouse. I was nervous, but excited. Tom had been hurt in an accident on his bike and could not attend. I expected to see Bernie and Doug, but they weren't there. Larry, whom I hadn't really spoken with much before, said he was expecting me. He greeted me and introduced me to the other guys. They all appeared to be cool with me, and asked if I wanted a beer or a coffee before we took off. I actually had to take a leak, so I took them up on that. It was still pissing down rain when we took off for Port Dover.

I'm usually pretty tolerant of bad weather, but I remember that run as a shit ride. It got better as we met several other members at gas stations and coffee shops on the way. I rode close to, but behind, the full-patch members, as was the rule. We actually started having fun, but since Sunny's bike was a piece of shit, it kept us from getting too fast. It simply did not like the rain. It was then that I began to realize that some of the members were pretty irresponsible and lacked appropriate consideration for others. Seriously, you should not attend a run if your bike is less than 100 percent.

A few weeks after Port Dover I went on a graveyard run, and Bernie took me and some others to the Woodbridge clubhouse for the after-run barbecue. The food I ate that day would soon become the staple diet for the rest of my biker career: overcooked sausages, stale buns and warm beer out of a Solo cup that I paid way too much for.

On our way there, the Ontario Provincial Police's Biker Enforcement Unit (BEU) had set up a roadblock as something of a welcome for the guests. It was my first time dealing with the BEU. Their attitude— license, insurance and shut the fuck up—would soon become very familiar.

At the next church meeting, Larry Pooler said he noticed that the officer who read my paperwork did not have a lot of questions for me. He wanted to know why. He was wondering why the cops wouldn't want to know everything they could about the new guy riding with the Para-Dice Riders. Usually, new guys get a major grilling from the cops. Tom defended me by saying that it was because the cops knew exactly who the fuck I was because they had arrested me before. That wasn't true, but it got Larry off my back. Luckily, I had attended a few parties by that time and the rest of the club recognized me as a good guy and a survivor (someone who could drink and party all day and night and still stand on his own two feet at the end)—that was important to them.

If I saw a member around town away from the clubhouse or club functions, he would always be polite and greet me, but he'd stay at arm's length. I got in shit once because I was greeted by a member and replied with the name I knew him by: Karl. He really went off on me for using his real name in public. I had no idea they were so secretive about that sort of thing. To make it up to him, and get back in his good graces, I drove him twenty miles to a strip joint and hotel, waited all night for him to party and fuck, then drove him to his house the following morning. It was the middle of winter, so I hope he had a good time while I got cold sitting outside in the car.

I was still working full-time as a bodyguard while I was a Para-Dice Riders associate. I was even licensed with the OPP as a private investigator. I guess the police hadn't put two and two together yet. But I knew they would eventually, so I told my boss at Intercon that I planned to become a member of the Para-Dice Riders. I was surprised to learn that he had no problem with it. We were both pretty naive to think it wouldn't come back to bite me on the ass.

Since biker associates are such a big blip on police radar, they have to think about alcohol consumption and drug use in a different way because they get pulled over more than usual. Before I became an associate, I was never pulled over, but once I was one, it became a regular occurrence.

For me, being an associate meant being on the fringe of the club. It was okay, but it was not nearly enough. I have always been against doing anything half-assed. The way I look at it, either you're in all the

THE HARD WAY OUT

way or you're out. I did not volunteer for the club to be a wannabe.

It was about then that I was promoted to friend. It might not sound like much of a title, but a friend carries a little weight and has some new rights and privileges. It's still a step below a hangaround, who has a very definite set of rights, privileges and responsibilities.

If these names sound familiar, it's because 99 percent of all biker clubs base their structure on the Hells Angels' successful formula, and the Para-Dice Riders were no different. Some clubs change it up a little. The Bandidos, for example, like to give all their titles a Spanish-sounding flair. So what most clubs call a sergeant-at-arms, the Bandidos call a *sargento de armas*.

Once you are a friend, you have officially begun your journey to becoming a member—it's referred to as "being on the program."

A friend of the club is an individual who has declared his desire to eventually become a full-patch member. There is no set time period for the friend status; it can last as long as the person wants it to. However, the friend has to be sponsored by two full-patch members who have been in the club for at least one year.

When they have a candidate in mind, the sponsors announce in a church that they have a guy who wants to get on the program. They will give some background information if the guy is new to the chapter, and then bring the candidate up to the front of the room. Some members might ask questions. At this point, it's still all light-hearted and fun. After all, the members don't want the guy to run off before they've had a chance to abuse him.

The friend has to be accepted by the chapter. That is done by a show of hands. After a while, I began to notice that members generally put their hands up very slowly and cautiously when voting, trying to get a sense of which way the other guys were going.

If he's successfully voted in, the new friend will get a key to the front door of the clubhouse, be allowed behind the bar, work security shifts, have assigned tasks and or responsibilities around the clubhouse, like chores and shopping. If a visiting member shows up in town, the friend will often get a call to pick him up. At this point, the friend has no patches or clothing that identify the club. The friend does not need to have a motorcycle, but will be named on the chapter's club phone number card. The card is passed out to members throughout the world. The friend also gets a club card to identify himself to others in the biker world. The friend has a specific way of introducing himself to members; it's an introduction that is mandatory and very formal. The friend must introduce himself by his name or nickname and follow it with "friend of," then the chapter he is with, and combine it with the club's signature handshake. For example, I was Shaky Dave, friend of Downtown.

Every biker has to have a nickname. We rarely use each other's real names, and never in public. Mine came when one of the full-patch members said my chances of making it through the process were "shaky at best." He was joking, but it stuck. From that point on, I was Shaky or Shaky Dave to everyone involved with the club.

The members usually treat friends with gentle authority, watching, helping and advising—nothing too heavy. The friend will receive his instructions or jobs from a hangaround, which is the next rank closer to a member. Friends are not allowed in meetings, but otherwise have free run of the clubhouse and the offices, including computers and binders full of the club's records and data.

Not all clubs have the friend position, and even those that do don't force their supporters to become one. It's really just a feeling-out process that allows the club and the candidate to get to know each other better.

After he has proven his worth to the club, the friend and his sponsor will have a discussion about whether the friend wishes to continue on the program. When that day comes, the friend will stand in front of the chapter again, and announce that he wishes to be a hangaround. The full-patch members of the chapter will determine, by a show of hands, if they feel he is worthy of that position.

After the candidate has completed one year as a hangaround, his sponsor and the chapter's secretary will bring up his vote to step up to prospect status. The members will discuss how the hangaround has contributed around the clubhouse and how he has interacted with other members from support clubs and non-members. In this part of the process, some members can get very vocal. Most have a vested interest in the vote. Since the hangaround will be one step closer to becoming a member, and since most motorcycle clubs have major secrets and security issues, they have to be careful.

And there's tons of money to be made once you're in a motorcycle club. It's like having an American Express card with no limit, no interest and an option not to pay the balance. When I was a full-patch member, I didn't mind having a hangaround and friends of the club doing chores and cleaning up, but wearing the same patch as me, well, I took that very seriously. He had better be worth it.

Other members had other concerns, often protecting their chapter's security and its activities in the underworld.

There is no guarantee that after a year as a hangaround, the candidate will get promoted. And, unlike a friend, who can remain a friend for as long as he wants, a hangaround is in the process of becoming a full-patch member, often as soon as he can.

As with every step toward becoming a member, the hangaround will eventually be called up during a church meeting, stand in front of the entire chapter and have his performance audited. Every member can and may contribute, but only the president speaks directly to the hangaround.

If a hangaround passes the vote, he becomes a prospect. The prospect period lasts a minimum of one year. Prospects have significantly more rights and privileges than hangarounds, but also more responsibilities. They actually do most of the heavy lifting for the club. It's a lot of work, but on the street, being a prospect for a club has major weight. People, even those not affiliated with any club, know that a prospect has proven himself to other members and street guys. They know that he can take care of himself and won't back down. One of the primary responsibilities of a prospect is to inform full-patch members of concerns he has on the street. The member can then either address the problem or tell the prospect to stop bitching about it, man up and take care of it himself.

The official rule is that prospects can only be asked to do club business. That means a prospect must attend all functions and runs and must oversee chores and shopping for the clubhouse. Prospects will often get hangarounds and even friends to do the work; it doesn't matter as long as it gets done.

In reality, prospects are required to do anything a member tells them to do. And members can be as fussy, picky and petty as any diva. Sometimes they'll have broken shoelaces they need the prospect to replace, or they will say they can't afford gas for their bike, so they need the prospect to shell out for it. I've seen full-patch members whine like little girls just because the clubhouse fridge had the wrong brand of mayo.

But things were different for me. When I started on the program, there was no friend or hangaround position for me. I was immediately made a striker for the Para-Dice Riders. A striker is basically the same level as prospect, so Tuck and I gained some respect straight away. When I first got my vest, it had nothing on the back. That's how it starts. Then, as a prospect, you are allowed to get the bottom rocker, or little guy, which identifies the club's territory. Only members can wear the top rocker, or big guy, and the club's crest— that's why they are often referred to as full patches.

While I was a Para-Dice Riders prospect, the biker world changed. Before 1999, when the Hells Angels were considering patching over a club, they would make the club's members prospect just like a would-be member would have to. But Hells Angels national president Walter Stadnick had a plan to make the Hells Angels a dominant coast-to-coast club and offered a number of Ontario clubs Hells Angels membership without any prospecting period whatsoever. The Para-Dice Riders was one of them. You'd simply swap whatever patch you had for a highly coveted Hells Angels patch. Nothing like it had ever been done before, anywhere.

I immediately went from being a striker with the Para-Dice Riders to being a Hells Angels prospect. In the biker world, that's an immense promotion.

Like a lot of clubs that had to prospect for the Hells Angels membership, the guys in Manitoba resented us bitterly. They thought we had it too easy. Soon after our patch-over, Manitoba chapter president Ernie Dew and his heavy hitters from Winnipeg came for a visit.

Dew spent most of his time in Toronto nitpicking about this or that. And while most guys would just grab a Blue or a Canadian, he insisted upon drinking paralyzers, an effete mixed drink for high school girls that requires crushed ice, three kinds of booze, cola and milk.

I knew that Manitoba was a war zone, and always has been for clubs and street crews, so I understood their resentment. But the younger guys who came up through the ranks from the Zig Zag Crew, Manitoba's Hells Angels support club, did not resent us guys in Ontario, so I thought, *Fuck it*. They were the future out there anyway and I made Dew all the girlie drinks he wanted.

While I was a prospect trying to learn how to be a biker, the full patches were bikers trying to learn how to be Hells Angels. They had no idea what they were doing and clearly did not know the difference between a striker and a prospect. While a striker can be asked to do anything from raking a member's leaves to changing the oil in a member's wife's car or cleaning the clubhouse, a prospect can only do club-related chores. So Hells Angels full patches from other regions of Canada tended to treat me with more respect than members of my own region. Donny Petersen knew the difference. Don was always a quick study and very smart. He asked me to do very little—only club stuff, meeting stuff, cool stuff.

My year went by without a problem, and in September 1999 I stood in front of about ninety members of the Para-Dice Riders for my audit. They asked me if I had ever belonged to any other clubs. They asked what I knew about guns, and if I had a criminal record (I didn't). They asked if I worked, was married, had kids or owed money on the street. The questions are designed to filter out potential members who might be attempting to infiltrate the club as informants or for protection because they owe on the street.

When they were finished, I was asked to wait outside until church was over. When they came out, I learned that I had been promoted from hangaround to prospect. I socialized with other members for a while after that. We had a few beers, they took down my number and we made plans to ride to some more parties and events. It was all very cool.

Jason Tuck is still a full-patch member of the Hells Angels as I write this. His sponsors, Jake and Josh Neal, were his childhood friends. He was smart, quiet, good-looking and strong. Well-built and with a great sense of humor, he was exactly what they were looking for.

Paul "Sunny" Braybrook, the thirty-year member and former sergeant-at-arms who was busted down to striker, died in a motorcycle accident in 2005.

Tow Truck Tony was a drug addict and a fall-down waste of a human life. He was a striker for a week or two after that and was then sent on his way.

Ray Bonner was sponsored by Steve "Tiger" Lindsay, or maybe his brother, Russell. Ray did well, and is still a member in good standing with the Woodbridge Hells Angels. He was convicted along with Lindsay in an extortion case in 2005.

My first three weeks as a striker were very busy. I worked my security job, rubbing elbows with bankers and corporate execs and seeing to their needs, and on my days off, I was hanging out with the members of the Para-Dice Riders Toronto, attending parties and then doing the clubhouse chores.

My first time cleaning the clubhouse, I was washing the leather couches after a member, Mongrel John, brought back a stripper who had crabs. John was good about it, and he actually did some of the work himself. To tell you the truth, Tuck and I were pretty taken aback by the whole thing. We had no experience with crabs other than ordering them at Red Lobster.

All strikers are required to carry antacids, condoms, rolling papers, lighters, matches and all the members' phone numbers. Every once in a while, members will ask strikers to roll them a joint. I was hopeless at rolling joints. Steve "Dirtbag" McDonald spent a few days partying with me and did his best to try to show me how to roll, but I never caught on. I honestly tried. The effort was there, but the results weren't. Bobbo from Woodbridge also tried to teach me, but he was nowhere near as patient as Dirt was. To tell the truth, I never really learned.

After about eight weeks of striking with the Para-Dice Riders, it was very clear to me that my pals who sponsored me into the club, like TC, Doug Myles and Billy Dawson, were not your typical outlaw motorcycle club members. Sure, they did biker shit—they partied, they did drugs, they sold drugs, they rode and they represented—but there was a difference between them and other members. Some of the other members were far more hardcore: lifelong criminals who needed the club as protection or to boost their underworld networking.

One night in November 1999, after our weekly church meeting, Chapter President Neal gave Tuck and me our dice patches to be worn on our vests. Our vests already had a patch on the back that said "Striker" with two dice over top. But the patches he gave us were white on black and about six inches by six inches square— maybe even bigger. *Wow*, we both thought, *that's cool.*

Two weeks later, I was called to a meeting at Doug Myles's garage. When I got there, I saw that Tom and Bully were already there. The purpose of the meeting was to let me know that, over the last month or so, the Hells Angels had been proposing a patch-over. They told me that almost every club in Ontario was going to be patching over to Hells Angels. The Para-Dice Riders had put it to a vote, and the majority were in favor of becoming Hells Angels. That split the club in half. The loyalists offered me the choice of staying on as a Para-Dice Riders prospect (Jughead would sponsor me because Tom, my original sponsor, voted to patch over), or going to the Hells Angels' program as a prospect.

My first question was whether I had to kick up 10 percent of what I made. My second question was whether I'd have to kill anyone. Believe it or not, every biker worries about that. There's a lingering fear that you'll be ordered to off some guy, maybe a rival drug dealer, maybe some guy who ripped off a member. And murder was at the front of everyone's minds as soon as the Hells Angels came into the conversation. We had just seen them go to war in Quebec and watched as 180 or so people died. We knew that many Quebec Hells Angels rose through the ranks because of their body counts, and we were all afraid that we would have to do the same thing.

The answer to both questions was no. Doug said that nothing would change, only our patches. He assured us that we would still be autonomous. Tom said it would be the only smart choice, because after the mass patch-over, there would be nothing but Hells Angels left in Ontario.

He was not entirely right about that. The Vagabonds were among the few Ontario clubs that did not patch over. Their president tried a sneaky, end-around play by going to Montreal and promising the entire club to Stadnick and the Hells Angels. But he forgot one thing—to get a vote from the members. Once they found out, the rest of the Vags resisted any invitation from Hells Angels, and they threw President Peter "Crow" Lordon out, along with five of his fart catchers.

Of course, only a small minority of the Para-Dice Riders were the 1-percenters the Hells Angels were actually looking for. Tom certainly was, and for him it was Hells Angels or nothing. He knew that once they arrived in numbers, they would control all the dope, its quality and price, in Ontario. Some of the Para-Dice Riders guys had already made a lot of money in the coke trade, and they had Stadnick to thank for it.

Years ago, when the Hells Angels were still expanding through English-speaking Canada and fighting a bloody war in Quebec, members of the Para-Dice Riders and Vagabonds made a pact never to deal with the Hells Angels. They didn't want to get steamrolled by the big guys, and they certainly wanted no part of the violence they had seen in Montreal. The Vags had certainly not forgotten that their one-time president, Donald "Snorkel" Melanson, had taken two bullets to the back of the head after he'd fallen into debt with the Montreal Hells Angels back in 1987.

But Billy Dawson, the guy who said from jail that he'd sponsor me, had been buying coke off Stadnick for years. And, in a move that spoke to Stadnick's particular brand of expertise, they got away with it for years without anyone knowing. In their communications, they always referred to kilos of cocaine as "strippers." Since every-one knows that Quebec exports strippers all over the world, that the Hells Angels are involved in the adult entertainment business and that hiring dancers is not a crime, law enforcement and even other bikers thought the two were running a perfectly legal, if not entirely family-friendly, business moving strippers from Quebec to Ontario. I even saw it reported in a newspaper.

Although I was in no position to say anything, I definitely had mixed feelings about the patch-over. I actually knew Stadnick because I often drove him around when he was in the Toronto area. He was quiet, almost never wore his colors and didn't visit too many other bikers—he was strictly business.

But I had seen his work. For years, he had been courting clubs all over Canada, and there had been blood. Manitoba had been the worst because he had pitted Los Brovos and the Spartans against each other for his favor. The two clubs, which had lived in peace for decades, were suddenly at war. We saw there that even brothers from the same mother would kill one another over a patch.

And it was personal for me. My mom's cousin was killed during the Quebec biker war. He was a twin, and they were targeting his brother and killed him by mistake.

But, like I said, I didn't have much of a choice. It was either sign on or go home. So, like all the other guys, I had to pack all my Para-Dice Riders stuff in a bag and turn it in at the clubhouse. I was sad to see that so many of the guys used garbage bags. It just didn't seem right.

New Year's Day—January 1, 2000—ushered in more than just a new year, decade, century and millennium. It also marked the beginning of my new life. From now on, for better or worse, I was a Hells Angel. There was no turning back.

6

PLAYING IN THE BIG LEAGUES

Being with the Hells Angels is not like being with the Para-Dice Riders. There are bikers, and then there are Hells Angels. Everybody, including cops, other bikers, women, everybody—looks at you differently when you're wearing the death's head patch. You get a lot of respect. And it's a different life. It's more than being part of a club; it's a job, it's a career, it's a lifestyle. To put on the Hells Angels patch is to get something very rare and very valuable—something a precious few have ever experienced—but something that also comes at great cost.

After the meeting in Doug's garage where we discussed the looming patch-over, it became essential for everyone involved in the Para-Dice Riders to declare their loyalty and their intentions. I took a giant leap of faith and said that I would remain with my sponsors and take their side in becoming Hells Angels.

That, of course, meant that I could no longer wear my Para-Dice Riders stuff anymore. Not surprisingly, the presence of two sets of bikers led to some very uncomfortable encounters within the clubhouse as loyalists bedecked in their Para-Dice Riders regalia and us soon-to-be Hells Angels in our jeans and T-shirts shared the same space for three weeks. Everybody knew who was who and where their loyalty lay.

People who haven't been in a motorcycle club really don't know what it's like. Once someone becomes a member, the club becomes the foundation of every facet of his life. It's his whole identity. Every shirt he puts on, every word that comes out of his mouth has to be in support of the club. He is the club's representative, and must behave accordingly. And a big part of that is his vow to support his brothers in the club, with his life if necessary, without question.

So the split led to a great deal of tension in the clubhouse as guys who thought they would live and die together as Para-Dice Riders were sharing the space with former brothers who had pledged their allegiance not just to another club and set of symbols, but a different set of brothers.

No small part of the rift came from the disruption of businesses—both criminal and legitimate—and investments. Many partnerships that had been built with years of hard-won trust were suddenly put into jeopardy. For years, the members of the Para-Dice Riders had paid their dues, bought property and established their territory together. The fracturing of the club was almost like a divorce—lines had to be redrawn, property divided as equitably as possible and disputes settled or allowed to simmer.

It all came down to a vote at church. Unlike many other clubs, who voted either to join or refuse the Hells Angels' offer as a club (and who often chased off any members who disagreed with the majority), our club allowed those who wanted to become Hells Angels to patch over and those who wanted to remain Para-Dice Riders to do so. Whichever side was in the majority would keep the clubhouses, the marina they had bought and all other real property, while the minority would be given the cash equivalent of their share of the value.

I was not allowed inside the meeting because I was still a striker, but it was pretty obvious which way things had gone after the members came filing out. The Hells Angels supporters had won the majority and the remaining Para-Dice Riders would have to find a new home. I never found out how much they were paid, but I knew they thought it was too little and many of them parted bitterly.

At the next church, the first I was invited into, we took all of our Para-Dice Riders stuff—vests, T-shirts and everything else—and piled it on the floor in the clubhouse. We then packed it all in plastic garbage bags to be sent to the remaining Para-Dice Riders. It was, by all rights, theirs and we had no use for it anymore. *Imagine that*, I thought at the time. All the years of loyalty, arrests, divorces, jail, parties, runs and both good and bad times were being disposed of in fucking green garbage bags. Nobody spoke. Despite the mundane tasks, it was a solemn occasion.

Jason Tuck and I took some of the Para-Dice Riders stuff to one of the remaining members. I forget who it was exactly, but I do remember it was a very cold interaction. I'm sure it was no better when their strikers came by what was now our clubhouse to pick up the rest of the stuff later in the week.

And that's about the time the big news came. After an officers' meeting, Doug told me that we were all going to the Hells Angels' unofficial national headquarters in Sorel, Quebec, to get our patches.

To this point, my life as a striker had been relatively quiet. There had been plenty of backdoor meetings—Para-Dice Riders members would meet with certain Satan's Choice members often, and used to meet just as frequently with the Vagabonds—but that stopped once the other clubs caught wind of our change in allegiance. The Vags had to keep their oath to avoid the Hells Angels, and they would no longer invite us to their parties or accept the invitations we extended to them.

The guys hired a bus to take us all to Sorel for the ceremony. But I didn't actually go on the bus because a member named Dave Blackwood slowed us down and we missed it. It was just as well. From what I heard, the guys who took it were not acting like themselves. They were all nervous, excited, worried and anxious. Fuck that.

Instead, Blackwood and I drove to Sorel. On the way, we picked up John Gray, who we knew better as Johnny G. We always called him that because we didn't want to confuse him with the other John Gray, who we called Johno and who later became president of the Woodbridge chapter before passing away after a motorcycle accident in 2005. They could hardly have been more different. Johno was a giant, six foot five and more than three hundred pounds, while Johnny G was a runt—we called him a dwarf. Johnny G was an irritating little ball of annoyance with a high, grating voice and a laugh that could set your teeth on edge. And, because he had just returned from a holiday in Mexico, he also missed the bus.

We were on our way to Quebec in late December, so we naturally drove through one fuck of a snowstorm. And we got lost. That was pretty typical for Blackwood—he never could do much right. He was a Newfie, a great guy, a tough guy, but he got way too involved in clubhouse drama for his own good.

In the middle of the blinding snow, we knew we had gone the wrong way and much too far. I spotted a cop sitting in his car on the roadside near Sherbrooke, and got Blackwood to stop to ask him for directions to Sorel. The cop didn't speak much English, but between Blackwood's broken French and my even worse attempts, we got it all figured out. Believe it or not, the cop was very helpful in our metamorphosis from Para-Dice Riders into Hells Angels.

Once we got to Sorel, finding the clubhouse was not a big deal. All we had to do was follow the flashing red lights on top of all the police cars.

Thinking ourselves to be cleverly covert, we parked around the corner. I was actually kind of relieved to see an Ontario copper that I knew in front of the clubhouse. George Cousens from the Ontario Provincial Police Biker Enforcement Unit and a number of other Ontario cops had made the trip so that they could photograph Ontario members marching into the fortified clubhouse as worried, anxious and patch-less bikers, later coming out with their chests puffed out with pride as Hells Angels. Some of the cops tried to mock us for being disloyal to our old clubs, but we paid no attention to them. We were Hells Angels now. As one cop I knew put it, it's like being called up from the American Hockey League to the NHL.

Hanging out with Blackwood was a lot of fun, but when he could have stood up for me, he didn't, and I never forgot that. Another member, Carl Stoyan, started heating me up, giving me shit for not being on the bus. When I tried to explain what had happened, he then gave me shit for blaming a full-patch member when I was just a striker. I failed that test on two counts. The dressing-down mercifully ended when the president, John "Winner" Neal, told me to report to a Quebec prospect and get to work at whatever chores the hosts wanted me to do.

The outside didn't look like much, but the inside of the Sorel clubhouse was an awesome man cave. It was multi-leveled with a gym, showers, indoor parking areas with vans and cars. As we were walking past the vehicles, I couldn't help but tell Lou, another member, that I wondered if they were the same ones used in what the media was calling the Sherbrooke Massacre when the Hells Angels killed five of their own members over drug debts back in 1985. Lou admitted that he had been thinking the same thing. It made me gulp and choke a little.

We went up a flight of stairs into a room that was filled with a team of seamstresses working on industrial-sized sewing machines. One of the ways the Hells Angels are different from other clubs is their attention to detail. The patches had to be sewn in a precise position, with each corner an exact distance away from the others.

I was ordered to get in line. Members from all over, who knew I was not yet a full patch, cut in front. Later, when a member asked why it had taken so long for me to get my prospect patch sewn on, I simply pointed at the line, which by then was running up the stairs and well into the bar area. He laughed and gave me shit for not letting our own full-patch members go in front of me.

Some of the guys couldn't wait to show off their new colors, prancing around from bar to bar, letting everyone know who they were. But my own Hells Angels career started with me working all night, cleaning tables, getting drinks and food for the full patches. Luckily, I got to know a Montreal member who was kind enough to slip me a half-gram of blow. That won me great respect with members from Ontario who needed a bump or two. The whole experience had been long and hard, kind of like math class.

When Dave, Johnny G and I headed out the next day, there was another snowstorm. At least Dave knew the way this time. For most of the trip, thankfully, John slept. I prayed because Dave drove like the kind of guy who did not realize accidents happen more frequently in storms. My ass clenched so hard, it bit the seat on more than one occasion. The prick dropped me at the clubhouse so I could get to work again. At least this time it was on my terms, without anyone looking over my shoulder.

For our first church meeting as Hells Angels, we arranged for a club photo night. Everyone showed up with their new patches, and some guys even wore Hells Angels T-shirts they had picked up in Quebec.

I had been at the clubhouse all day, working. We were busy replacing the Para-Dice Riders' black-and-white theme with the red-and-white theme of the Hells Angels. That meant we had to paint everything, including the display cases, which involved taking down plaques and trophies from the Para-Dice Riders days. A few things stayed, but nothing that sported the old Para-Dice Riders logo or name prominently.

I sat at the end of the bar and watched as the members walked in for the first time as Hells Angels. I couldn't help but laugh to myself as I watched them imitate what they had seen in Quebec. Guys who had spent their whole lives in Levi's or jeans from Mark's Work Warehouse had packed that look in, trading up for designer gear. And guys cut their hair too. Stadnick wanted us all to look more like gentlemen than bums. Dirtbag, who became a road partner of mine on a few runs, had totally reinvented himself with short, tidy hair, nice shoes and shirts. He'd always had some style, but now he was what we called "Quebec classy." Some members took it to ridiculous extremes. They were the same guys who would talk in fake French accents when Quebec members would visit. I still wonder if they thought it would help the Quebeckers understand English better. Even if it did, I was embarrassed for them.

As the weeks dragged on with me as a prospect, I began to realize that there were two types of members: low-maintenance and high. Some members would ask for nothing, while others never left you alone. If I was not at the clubhouse and those members with not much going on in their lives were there, they would page me to go get them a burger, a coffee, a ride or whatever else they felt like. Others I would never hear from unless it was church night. On those nights, I would run around picking up members, dropping off members, getting burgers. And it was never just a burger, those pricks always wanted special orders. And if you got it wrong, they did their best to make you feel like an idiot.

They didn't see it that way in Quebec. Since I was a prospect who had already spent his time as a striker, I was more than a gofer and, they thought, deserved a little respect. When legendary Quebec biker Paul "Sasquatch" Porter came by to introduce himself, he made that clear. Porter had been a leader with the SS and the Rock Machine, and had found his way into a leadership position with the Hells Angels as president of the Ottawa Nomads chapter. Even among us bikers, Paul was a giant. I don't know any exact numbers, but I would describe him as the size of a Kenworth with a mountain added on. He carried himself with a quiet confidence that made him seem even bigger and more important that he actually was.

But he was also friendly to me and very sociable in general. He said he respected Tuck and me because we were working hard to earn our Hells Angels patches. It didn't take a brain surgeon to realize that he was intimating that most of the guys who had patched over recently would never be able to earn a Hells Angels patch on their own. I couldn't help but think that guys from Winnipeg were particularly strong examples of that kind of thinking.

While Paul was there, Bobbo Gray from Woodbridge ordered me to go grab him a burger from a nearby steak joint on Queen Street. He was not clear about what he wanted on it, and for fuck's sake, it's just a burger—if it's short a condiment, add it, and if it's got one you don't want, take that shit off. Well, I quickly found out that mustard and Bobbo don't get along at all, and he gave me proper shit in front of all the guests and members. If I hadn't been a prospect trying to get 100 percent support to become a full patch, I would not have let him get away with it. It was nothing but schoolyard bullying, and he knew there was fuck all I could do about it.

To my utter surprise, Sasquatch started giving Bobbo major shit. And he made sure that everyone could hear it too. "Dave is a prospect, and he will be your brother soon," he said. "Dave is young and strong and will fight for you in years to come." Then he added, with obvious disgust, "You are a Hells Angel now; you treat every-one with respect until they treat you with disrespect." Being dressed down like that in front of everyone left Bobbo absolutely speechless. After overcoming his initial shock, Bobbo spat the burger out and whined. That was a mistake because it made him look even more like a crybaby bitch.

My only thought was, "*Fuckin' right, Sasquatch.*" But when I discussed it with Tuck, he pointed out that Paul would eventually leave, but Bobbo was here for good. I might have been a prospect, but I was his prospect, not Paul's, so I had better watch my Ps and Qs. Tuck was always a pretty wise dude.

After the patch-over and a few weeks of church under our belts (red leather belts, in fact, with huge death's head buckles that had been given to us by the club), the chapter became aware of the increased importance of club parties. As a biker, riding to cold beer, a burger on a fresh bun and some titties to look at was common prac-tice, enjoyed by all riders, whether they were 1-percenters or just weekend warriors. What we learned was that through rain, snow, sleet or hail, Hells Angels parties are a mandatory way of spending week-ends. And they are expensive. Every weekend, one or more chapters were having parties.

Before the patch-over, it was all easy and fun: Halloween party at the Vags, Christmas at the Para-Dice Riders. Fridays were reserved for Satan's Choice, and Saturday could be the Vags or the Para-Dice Riders. All very simple. But after the Hells Angels had taken over, there was a party every weekend—and it could be in Simcoe County or even Windsor. We'd have to drive for three or more hours, pay $20 to get in, then $20 or more for a few beer tickets. The full-patch members started complaining about that. But within a few months, we all realized that to be a Hells Angel, you had to travel and you had to pay.

The guys in Winnipeg were having a party for their first anniversary as Hells Angels. Most of our guys flew out, prospects included. Even though we weren't exactly friends, we were brothers, so we were expected to go. My sponsors chipped in for my ticket because having a legitimate job actually prevented me from making as much money as the other guys.

The trip wasn't that bad, actually; the guys behaved at the airport, and there was not a great deal of police presence. We went low-profile, with our vests in bags and regular clothes on our backs. Still, we looked like what we were—a big group of bikers. After a quick plane ride, we were picked up at the airport by Winnipeg hangarounds, prospects and even a few members. There were so many bikers there that several shuttles were needed to take us all to the party.

We quickly learned about the first-class style the Hells Angels use to treat their guests. We paid for our own drinks and food, and we were shuttled from bar to bar, strip joint to strip joint. I rarely even had a beer in my hand.

We were mostly handled by the Zig Zag Crew, the Hells Angels' support club in Winnipeg. I took my instructions from one of them, Dale "Deli" Donovan. He was young, tall and tough, and he was well connected. He ran a lot of the neighborhoods near where he lived. When Deli had some errands to run, he asked me to come along. Despite our age difference and upbringing, we connected. Years later he would become president of the Winnipeg chapter.

The party went on all night, and I was serving drinks until the end, and cleaning up afterward. When it was time to fly home, our chapter met in the lobby and the sergeant-at-arms, Mark "Magic" Dafoe, whose responsibility it was to protect us all, could not find Russell Lindsay. Both Mark and Russ were hardcore tough guys. They were no-nonsense men who treated women with respect but kept them at arm's length. In fact, they treated everyone with respect. But if they were ever disrespected, by anybody, they would react accordingly, usually with a smack to the mouth.

I had a list with everyone's room numbers and a card key for Russ's room. Under orders from Magic, I headed up to Russ's room. When I announced myself and entered, no one answered. The tub was running and Russ was in it, unconscious. The tub was full and was draining through the overflow hole under the tap. I could see Russ's head bobbing on the surface. He was still breathing, but very close to drowning. I quickly pulled the drain plug and tilted his head away from the water. I tried in vain to wake him, but he was out cold. He was a hard-drinking, hard-partying man and had just gone too far the night before. Eventually, Magic appeared. He assisted me, or rather, I assisted him in getting Russ ready to fly back home.

When asked by other members what had happened, I said very little. I did tell my sponsors later. They commended me and told me that's what being a good brother is all about. Russ and I had always gotten along. He was in charge of security when meetings were held and other officers flew in. Russ counted on me to be one of the drivers and to hang around at the location of each meeting, providing another set of eyes, ears and muscle.

In the first year after the patch-over, Hells Angels from Quebec would come to visit. We knew they were checking up on us, and we were cool with that. They had made a huge investment in us guys in Ontario—for the most part, almost sight unseen—and wanted to make sure we weren't fucking up.

It was a big job. Overnight, Ontario had gone from having zero Hells Angels chapters to fourteen. Other than the two Para-Dice Riders chapters, who were relatively disciplined and organized, the other bikers, and the value these guys brought to the Hells Angels, varied widely.

Every Satan's Choice member either patched or quit the life. They buried the patch when they became Hells Angels, and the long and storied club—at one time rivaling the Hells Angels themselves in size and reach—ceased to exist. What was left of the Choice were the Hells Angels' Sudbury, East Toronto, Oshawa, Thunder Bay and Simcoe County chapters.

The West Toronto Hells Angels had been a gang called Last Chance. They were small and, unlike other clubs in the patch-over, claimed to be "clean and sober." But when they saw that the Bandidos had come to Ontario and were still unofficially at war with the Hells Angels from the time when they were known as the Rock Machine, they knew which side would come out on top and were eager to join.

The new Windsor chapter had been the Lobos (which they wrote as Lobo's on their patch). They had a reputation as being not all that bright—and had a number of unnecessary run-ins with the law that backed that up—but were considered valuable because of their proximity to the U.S. border.

The other new chapters—Niagara, Ottawa (they were designated as Nomads, which placed them a notch above the rest), North Toronto, Hamilton and London were new. Most of their members were former Outlaws or Bandidos who were reinforced with some guys from Quebec, but some of them were altogether new to the life. Niagara, which would grow to be one of the richest and more powerful chapters, was formed from a bunch of Stadnick's old coke-dealing buddies. Their president, Gerald "Skinny" Ward, actually had to be taught how to ride a motorcycle. They all knew that with the Hells Angels in Ontario, there would be no drug business at all for them if they didn't join.

Ontario members would fall over themselves trying to impress the visiting Quebec members. Some even learned a little French. But the main contenders for the Quebeckers' favorite clubhouse to visit were the old Para-Dice Riders chapters—which had become the Downtown Toronto and Woodbridge Hells Angels. We had no shortage of top strippers, fine dining and comfortable, well-appointed clubhouses. We knew the Quebec Hells Angels enjoyed fine wine, designer clothes and expensive watches, so we made sure they were able to get them when they came to Toronto.

One day, not long before the patch-over, Downtown Toronto was hosting a party at the clubhouse. Some Quebec members were there, but they seemed quiet and reserved. Earlier in the day, there had been meetings between the visiting members and Ontario officers in a vacant paint shop on College Street near Spadina Avenue.

The instructions from our chapter's sergeant-at-arms were to arrive at the clubhouse on time and sober, and to be sure not to wear anything that would identify us as Hells Angels. From there, we would pick up rental cars and take them to assigned venues to pick up a visiting member.

It was a rainy Saturday morning. I got to the paint shop and started setting up chairs in the basement. Mark Staples was already there. He had arranged the venue, meals and security. He owned a martial arts studio and was well spoken and polite to everyone. Years ago, Mark was very suspicious of one of our guys—and he was right to have been. The full patch was an agent working for OPP detective George Cousens. He would later write in his book, *Befriend and Betray*, under the name Alex Caine, that Mark once followed him right up to a meeting he was going to have with Cousens. I have to laugh about that now. For a guy like that, who shamelessly promotes what a pro he is at everything, he wasn't careful enough to prevent Mark from dusting his tail. He was burned.

Mark, on the other hand, was cautious and smart. After it all went down, it took the government a long time to toss him from the country for belonging to a crime organization and not being a Canadian citizen (he had moved from Scotland when he was six or seven, but he never got around to applying for citizenship). If we had not patched over to the Hells Angels, I'm certain Mark would still be in Canada. He would have been able to stay under the police radar.

As usual, the full-patch Ontario members wanted to keep the prospects running for coffee or food during the meeting. But Mark had arranged for it to be catered because it was a secret meeting and he thought it wise to keep all the guests contained. That, he thought, would prevent cops from getting wise and, of course, it would also keep everyone in the room and on the same timeline.

My instructions were to prevent anybody from going back upstairs and outside. Members would try to get in. That was funny to me, because I was required to say no way. Tiger from Woodbridge showed up, and he wasn't used to being told no—especially by a prospect/striker like me. I took great pleasure in seeing the look on his face as I said, "No, you're not allowed upstairs, and that's that." Of course, I knew I would pay for that insolence down the road, but I still took pleasure in telling the full-patch members attending the meeting they could not leave.

Stadnick came down at one point in the meeting and told me he was expecting two guests who would be allowed upstairs—Duane and Skinny from Niagara.

Despite what I had heard about him, Skinny looked like a biker. He had a barrel chest, a long, gray ponytail and a Harley jacket. Duane looked like a divorced father who was on his weekend without the kids. He was slender, tall, talkative and pleasant. He was the yin to Ward's yang.

When they showed up, I frisked them and took their cell phones and pagers. Yeah, guys were still using pagers back then. While we were waiting for Stadnick to come down to get them, we engaged in a little small talk. Skinny told me he had just finished a long stretch in jail, awaiting trial for a murder charge. I later found out that he was acquitted and spent less than two years behind bars.

Duane had the appearance of a businessman, for sure. He knew the real estate agent's basic rules of interaction: look someone in the eyes, share the conversation but contribute, be lighthearted and positive and respectful. It was easy to like Duane. We often spoke at parties, and, in my role as a prospect, I was always very quick to help him out.

Eventually, Stadnick came down to collect Duane and Skinny. He announced that they had gotten their prospective charter. They were our new Niagara chapter.

That meeting was the last time I ever spoke to Stadnick. As I was standing guard at the front door, he asked me what was up. We spoke about how Billy Dawson was in jail and that he would probably get out within the year. As always, Stadnick was very cordial and he engaged in conversation on current events easily. But, as I had seen before, if anyone tried to self-promote or talk about any illegal shit, he would just turn around and walk away without a word.

The trouble with bringing all these disparate groups of self-proclaimed outlaw bikers together under one patch is that they inevitably have history. Decades of bad blood, from drug rips to stolen girlfriends, were suddenly re-exposed. Old wounds were reopened. So anyone being brought into the fold after the patch-over required extensive negotiations to sort out any bad debts and other conflicts. Among the 250 guys who were brought in, there were a lot of toes that had been stepped on in the past. That was one of the reasons the Para-Dice Riders were so adamant about finding out if I owed money on the street when I started striking.

Duane and Skinny came down after an hour or more of being up in the secret meeting. Duane gave me the thumbs-up. We laughed, knowing that bikers were not supposed to get excited about things like that.

But we did. Of course we did. It was hard not to get caught up in the whole thing. Not only had we become Hells Angels, but the legendary club had just become dominant in Canada. The Hells Angels' dominion stretched from Atlantic to Pacific, and they were suddenly the big dogs in Ontario as well.

It was hard, at the time, for me to comprehend exactly how big a deal it was. But it really hit me when we were returning from a party in Winnipeg. On the flight home, everyone was quiet. It seemed that, no matter what it looked like, all of the members were still nervous about the patch-over. It was a tacit form of bonding, I guess.

When the plane touched down in Toronto, we filed out and down the ramp into the terminal. I was walking beside Doug when I glanced over and saw what looked like a number of soldiers staring at us. It was the Peel Regional Police's Tactical Response Team in full gear— helmets, vests, dark uniforms and long guns. They flanked us as we all made our way past the luggage carousel and out of the terminal.

Russell Lindsay was asked a question by one of them and he barked, "Fuck off." Russ was cool that way. I remember once, when we were in Winnipeg, our car got pulled over. One of the cops tried to open the door, and Russ shut it, telling the cop he couldn't legally do that and to fuck off as well. Russ was right: the cop could not do that. The driver had all his papers in order, he was photographed and let go.

Doug and I started chanting "hut-two-three-four, hut-two-three-four" as the cops escorted us right out of the airport. We were frequently photographed, by passersby as well as cops, as we waited for our ride.

That's when you know you've made it in the biker business. You take a little trip, and when you get home, there's a small army of cops with helmets and assault rifles there to meet you at the airport.

7

THE BIG CHANGE

I knew life would be different for me as a Hells Angel, but I didn't know exactly how different. After Walter Stadnick had managed to patch over so many bikers from so many clubs in so many cities, we former Para-Dice Riders were suddenly brothers with a disparate bunch of guys, most of whom we had never met. Along with them came their prospects, their hangarounds, their friends and associates. We had changed overnight from a bunch of guys who liked to ride, to party and maybe to break a few rules, into cogs in a huge, almost corporate machine whose purpose was to make money. We had changed from friends and brothers to business associates and employees.

After the patch-over in Sorel, we in Ontario suddenly outnumbered the other provinces when it came to Hells Angels. One newspaper—I forget which—even reported that southern Ontario had the greatest concentration of Hells Angels in the world, even more than southern California.

But the power was still in Montreal—at least for the time being. It was held tightly in the hands of people like Stadnick and Maurice "Mom" Boucher. Compared to hardcore drug dealers and gangsters like that, we looked like a bunch of schoolboys on mopeds. That would eventually change as we began to learn and put into practice the valuable lessons that Stadnick and his men would teach us. Playtime was over. Those of us in Ontario were real Hells Angels, and it was important to us to start doing things the right way.

The one thing everybody needed was a job. And by that, I don't mean some gig at a factory or office where you check in every morning and check out every night. I mean that every member had to show that he was of real, concrete value to the club as a whole.

Tattoo artists are particularly valued by clubs, especially the Hells Angels. Not only do bikers like to get, and sometimes are required to get, tattoos, it's a popular business in which almost all transactions are paid in cash. That makes it perfect for money laundering and other kinds of side deals. Of course, not all tattoo artists are into those types of deals, and I never saw our guys do anything like that, but it was well known that some did.

In Toronto, the club had three very talented tattoo artists—Dave "Psycho" Naughton, Steve "Dirtbag" McDonald and Phil Johnson. All three were perpetually in high demand.

Psycho had earned his nickname long before I met him. He was a pleasant-enough guy with me and we had some great times while I was a member. He was exactly what you'd expect of a Hells Angel with a tattoo business. When he wasn't inking people up, he was working out or partying hard. In fact, Psycho was so dedicated to the

life that he was one of the few bikers I ever met who had a motorcycle license but never had a license to drive a car. But he wasn't a
total hard-ass. An inner-city kid, he loved his family, his daughter
and his club, but he also liked to have a good time. And he, unlike
so many others, would rather have a laugh than a fight when things
got rough. He was a regular guy, easy to talk with, and we shared
many sincere conversations about bikes, women, drugs and all kinds
of other topics. Naughton was one of the guys I was actually looking
forward to spending time with once I was a member.

Dirtbag changed his name to DB after the patch-over, and I
didn't blame him, I would have too. Who wants to be known as Dirtbag? I got along pretty good with him as well. He was shorter—
maybe five foot nine—lightly built and older than me, and a decent
guy. He loved to ride and organized a run to the East Coast every
year. I always enjoyed going, and one of the reasons was that DB
knew every single place along the way where we could drink, fuck,
sleep and even get a decent bite to eat. It was always great fun. DB
and Psycho were usually riding partners on most runs, but if one of
them couldn't make it, I was more than happy to fill in for him. DB's
health began to fail him later on, but he never seemed to me to slow
down even a little.

The two of them ran a storefront operation in Etobicoke called
the Great Canadian Tattoo Company. It was always a pretty busy
place, in no small part because of DB's talent. He was a real artist
who could draw, paint and even make sculptures as well as make
tattoos. I know he studied art at Humber College, and I have been
told he taught a class in drawing there as well. He was very generous

with his knowledge at the shop too, helping young artists fine-tune their skills.

The other tattoo artist, Phil, was a big-time partier. He was also a mountain of a man, simply a massive dude who had a booming, raspy voice that made him seem even bigger than he was. Like Psycho and DB, he was covered in tattoos, but because of his size he probably had more ink under his skin than Psycho and DB combined.

In the biker world, colors mean everything. And now that we were Hells Angels, we were required to wear our colors. And because so many of us had become Hells Angels so quickly, we needed a lot of gear right away. We needed vests, jackets, T-shirts and jewelry.

Increasing the demand was the fact that Hells Angels love to buy gear from other chapters or, even better, receive them as gifts. It was a status symbol. Stadnick, of course, was at the forefront of that. One day, you'd see him in a T-shirt from the Sherbrooke chapter in Quebec and the next he would be wearing a T-shirt from the Bremen chapter in Germany.

So when any members visited another chapter, one of the first things they would do is buy some gear. I was no different, and I enjoyed showing off the gear I had acquired from other chapters.

(The only major exception was Manitoba. No matter how many times they came, they never seemed to buy any Ontario stuff. You can bet they were still sore over the fact that we patched over basically sight unseen while they had to go to war to win Stadnick's favor, and, even after all the killings there, they still had to put in a year of probation before they could call themselves Hells Angels. And it didn't help that it was becoming increasingly clear that we were gaining in power, and they were likely to become just another sidelined outpost again.)

And that doesn't even include support gear. The Hells Angels won't allow any non-member to wear their name or their winged-skull logo. There's a zero tolerance policy on that, and, in rare instances, the penalty for doing so can even be death. But the Hells Angels also have a huge number of friends, associates, well-wishers, old ladies and even fans who want to show their support. For them, there's support gear—clothes that indicate allegiance to the club without actually using its name or logo. They're usually, but not always, red and white and will use names like Big Red Machine or the number 81. If you don't get it, 81 comes from the fact that *H* is the eighth letter of the alphabet and *A* is the first, so 81 represents *HA*, for Hells Angels.

Not only does wearing support gear show a person's allegiance, but it can help them out in a scrape. If you are in a really tense situation, and your opponent sees that you're wearing support gear, he might think twice about throwing the first punch because he can never be all that sure who your friends are.

And it made us money. Tons of money. We sold everything, not just the T-shirts, hoodies and bandannas you might expect, but also bikinis, thongs and even baby clothes. Like I said, you'd be surprised at how many people in Ontario wanted to show their support.

So the three talented tattoo artists we had were working overtime to come up with enough menacing-looking designs for our own uses and support gear to satisfy all the new Hells Angels and the legions of supporters. But there was more to it than just flames, skulls and dragons. Every design had to follow specific quality-control rules. The Hells Angels were very choosy about how they were represented and who was allowed to wear what. And everything had to correspond to international copyright laws. That way, there was no mistake about who made what and where the money was going.

It didn't take long before we had our swag sorted out. What we had to get used to was the nonstop visitor traffic from other out-of-town members. When we were Para-Dice Riders, there would be parties every once in a while, but when we were Hells Angels, it was like Grand Central Station—all kinds of people were coming and going all the time.

And they were not just a bunch of guys hanging out and maybe having the odd Molson Canadian. We quickly found out that Quebec Hells Angels are not exactly a low-maintenance group of motorcycle riders. Most of the full-patch members had actually gotten rich and very quickly become used to the finer things in life, like expensive wine and five-star restaurants.

So we, as Ontario bikers, had to pick up our game. Of course, Toronto had some guys with real money. But they did not want to spend it entertaining dudes from other parts of the country. Even as a prospect, I could easily see the frustration our chapter's officers went through whenever a member from another chapter arrived at the clubhouse door, expecting to be wined and dined on their tab.

During the months after the patch-over, some of the Toronto members would travel to other regions and even countries—and not just to get a free meal. They would return with valuable information and brief the membership on the ways that other chapters were organized. One of the main things they talked about was the wide variation in how different chapters treated their prospects, hang-arounds and non-members.

Slowly, the Hells Angels way was being established in Ontario. But, like Stadnick had told us, it would take at least two years before Ontario would be running like a Hells Angels province.

But the Hells Angels way did not come easily to everyone. I saw a few members get kicked out for keeping to the old way of doing things instead of adapting to the new reality. One guy from West Toronto did too many nitrous oxide balloons at a party, got high and disoriented and fell face first into a pool table. He was out. Other guys would miss too many meetings or act like fools in other ways and get the boot.

The other thing that we had a hard time getting used to was how expensive it was to be a Hells Angel. Every weekend, someone was at our clubhouse or we were heading to another clubhouse to party. And that takes cash.

I knew there would be a point at which my two lives would collide. As a security guard, my job was to protect my clients, their families and their property. But if you really get down to it, I was actually enforcing a code of behavior on people, even if I did fudge the law just a little bit from time to time. That code was more than just "keep your hands off my client," it was more like "don't even think about it." And it took sternly applied discipline on my part, not just to do the job, but to do it right and stay out of trouble. Of course, there were some similarities to my life as a biker, even though most people would see security guards and bikers as being on opposite sides of the law. And simply wearing my colors was enough to make sure people kept their distance.

As I mentioned earlier, before I even started to strike with the Para-Dice Riders, I asked my boss at Intercon if it would be a problem if I joined the club. I wasn't sure how he'd react, but I did know that his half-brother, a guy named Doug, was a longtime Satan's Choice member. He later patched over to the Hells Angels with the rest of us.

My boss thought about it, and I remember his exact words to this day: "There is nothing illegal about belonging to a motorcycle club as long as you don't do anything like get charged for drugs or assault or any other criminal convictions—I don't see a problem with it."

So for a little while, at least, I managed to balance the considerable responsibilities of a striker along with being employed full-time as a high-level security guard. Seriously high-level. In fact, just after the patch-over, I was working for Intercon at a gala event in one of Toronto's poshest high-buck neighborhoods. The client I was protecting was hosting a lavish gala event at his home. The guest list that night read like a who's who of the Canadian elite at the time. There were plenty of corporate types, and there were also headliners like Aloysius Cardinal Ambrozic, world-renowned cellist Yo-Yo Ma and, perhaps a little farther down the list, the prime minister of Canada at the time, Paul Martin.

We didn't just provide security for the night of the party. The event was so big and the guest list so important that we spent the whole week leading up to the party making sure that the people preparing and organizing the arrival of tables, chairs, tents and caterers were seriously vetted. We certainly didn't want any danger coming from within.

Well before the first guest arrived, we worked out the logistics of how to best observe and protect those people serving and preparing food, the guys taking care of garbage removal, the valets who handled guest parking and even the sound people who ensured the acoustics were optimal for Yo-Yo's cello.

Because the guest list featured so many truly important people, the RCMP sent an advance team to perform a reconnaissance survey of the host's house and the surrounding neighborhood.

As someone who had made a career in security, with a particular interest in protecting important people, I was more than a little intrigued to find out how the top-of-the-line pros would protect someone like the prime minister. So I spoke with the RCMP advance team coordinator while we were both prepping for the big shindig. Much to my surprise, he was an okay guy, easy to deal with, but still very much a professional. He made a point of telling me that he was impressed by how diligent and thorough my coworkers and I had been when it came to keeping our client and his guests secure.

When the night of the party finally came, I was feeling pretty good about myself. We were running a tight ship. Everyone was accounted for, and no threats had arisen. So I was a little surprised when the RCMP liaison approached me with a concerned look on his face. "We don't have a serious problem," he told me. "But there is something I think you should be aware of."

Immediately, all of my protective instincts and security training came to the fore. I was more than just concerned; I was pumped and ready to act. We had important people in there, and I wanted to know right that second about any potential threat there might be.

119

The RCMP guy told me his people had done a neighborhood sweep, which included checking parked cars. They had run every plate in a twenty-block radius, and one had come back suspect.

I was freaking out. It was my job to protect these people, and I needed to know, immediately, exactly who posed a threat. I demanded to know what they had found.

It wasn't anything to be too alarmed about, he told me. It's just that one of the plates came back as belonging to a Hells Angel. Some guy named David Atwell.

I told him to look at the business card I had given him earlier. When he did, and I saw the shocked look on his face, I didn't know whether to laugh or get angry. In the end, all I could do was feel sorry for him (for missing the obvious).

Of course, he didn't speak to me for the rest of the evening.

It didn't sink in all at once. I was kind of proud of myself at first for showing up one of the country's top security experts, but I soon realized that the other shoe had yet to fall. After the patch-over, there had been a dramatic change in how I was being treated by cops, especially the OPP, and I knew that the RCMP would not make it easy for a Hells Angel to serve as security for some of Canada's wealthiest people. I knew, at that moment, that my membership was putting my entire career in jeopardy.

Later that week, I was called into my boss's office and had a long sit-down meeting with the manager of my division, who was actually my boss's boss. I had known the man since the mid-1980s, and I genuinely thought of him as a friend by that point. After all, we had gone through many battles in various shopping malls and had even made a training video together. I respected him, and I like to think he respected me.

I could tell it was serious, though. He told me that, earlier in the week, he had been paid a visit by the OPP's Biker Enforcement Unit (BEU). A couple of their officers came by to tell him that I had become a member of the Hells Angels. They also told him that meant I absolutely had to do anything the club told me to do, which could include kidnapping the very person I was protecting for Intercon.

I was in no position to argue with the man, let alone try to contradict him. I did, however, say that we both knew that would never happen. He agreed, but since the OPP were also in charge of private investigators' licenses, they had told him they were going to pull mine. A PI license isn't absolutely essential in my line of work, but it does help. I was relieved of my duties.

It was at this time that I realized exactly how serious the cops are when it comes to the Hells Angels, how serious the repercussions of being a member were going to be. I was on the radar of both the OPP and the RCMP, and I had already lost my job while I was still just a prospect.

Before I started as a striker with the Para-Dice Riders, when I was still just hanging out with the guys, both Doug Myles and Tom Craig had told me that three things would happen to me once I became a biker: I would lose my job, I would go to jail and I would lose my girl. I hadn't been a striker for very long, but one of their predictions had already come true. The other two seemed almost inevitable after that.

I went over to the clubhouse. I was feeling more than a little down and even a bit lost without my job. Working as a security guard had been a big part of who I was up to that point. I had been doing it since high school and it kind of felt like it was all I really knew. And it's not like word didn't get around in the small, tightly knit security community in Canada. Even if I somehow got another job, I knew it wouldn't take long for the BEU to send another couple of pricks to my new boss to tell him I was a Hells Angel and posed a bigger security risk than anyone I was watching out for. My career in security was over, and I was pretty bummed about it.

Once inside the clubhouse, one of the members asked me why I looked so disturbed. I told him that I had just lost my job. He laughed and said, "It's going to happen. What are you going to do?"

I realized then and there that I wouldn't get much sympathy from my brothers in the club. They just weren't built that way. Besides, civilian careers generally don't mean very much to most bikers. Few had any jobs of consequence, and some had never even worked a day of legitimate work in their lives.

But what I did get was a ton of phone calls from my former coworkers. I can summarize all of them in one sentence: "What the fuck were you thinking joining the Hells Angels?" I didn't know what to tell them.

I wasn't too bad off, actually. I had saved a pretty fair amount of cash and my girlfriend at the time, whose nickname was Bad Teri, was actually pretty sympathetic.

And that's when my next career move opened up.

Tom Craig dropped by and gave me two ounces of cocaine. It was all very just off the cuff, as natural as anything. He told me I could work for him if I wanted. I didn't really say I would; it just seemed inevitable. Tom was an old friend and an important guy. If he was doing me a favor, I was in no position to say no.

He told me to take the stuff to Rooster's, grab a couple of wobbly pops and the rest should take care of itself. The money I made, he assured me, would easily be enough to tide me over until something came up.

Rooster's Ribhouse was a popular barbecue-style restaurant and bar at the end of a strip mall on Kingston Road near the Scarborough neighborhood of West Hill. It was pretty basic inside—just a bar and some tables that groups would pull together to enjoy beer and wing specials—but there was a small deck that was nice and shady in the summer. The kitchen was clean and it was a good place to go if your idea of a hearty meal means one that's deep-fried.

It wasn't like Country BeBop's, which was usually occupied only by bikers and their associates. At any time, Rooster's could be full of a pretty diverse crowd, including teachers and blue-collar workers and, of course, bikers. The owner, a guy named Trevor, wasn't wild about having us hanging out there at first, but soon came around because real bikers—Hells Angels, yet—gave the place a little panache and allowed the other customers to "get their biker on." Besides, we spent a ton of money.

Trevor was a good guy, a Trinidadian. We always tried to get him to cook us up some traditional meals from his home country. Believe it or not, the guys in the chapter had become foodies of a sort, and all of us really enjoyed trying new foods from other cultures. Every once in a while, I'd get a call from one of the Rooster's staff telling me that Trevor had had a couple of shots of rum and had made his way into the kitchen. That was all I needed to hear to come running. I'd put the word out, and the next thing you knew, the place would be packed with bikers eager to get some of what we knew was going to be a first-class Trinidadian feast.

We were smart enough to follow the old maxim of not shitting where we ate, so we always treated the other customers at Rooster's with respect. Hell, we were polite almost to a fault.

Two of the waitresses at Rooster's were close to the club. Both of them were sexy, young and ambitious. Shanna was very refined, a tall, model type, and we were in what might be described as a relationship. But Penny was everybody's favorite. She was short and well built and a stripper when she wasn't waitressing, and she had a great deal of natural charm. She was funny, smart and a strong survivor. All the guys, even my dad, were crazy for her.

Penny had about half a dozen kids, and they all lived with her. After Rooster's closed for the evening, we'd often go to my place or Penny's for a few drinks. If we were at Penny's, it was normal for us to still be partying when the kids woke up for school. Sometimes, I'd be asleep on the couch and they'd wake me up. I'd crack a beer and help them with their homework and make breakfast, but once they were out of the house, I'd start partying again. I'd leave for the clubhouse, and Penny and Shanna would clean the house before heading off to work at Rooster's.

When I got there, I was greeted by Billy Dawson, who had recently gotten out of jail. He gave me $1,700 for each ounce and told me he would probably be able to move two or three every couple of weeks. It suddenly occurred to me that I had just moved two ounces of coke—that's about the weight of a golf ball—four blocks, handed it to a friend and made $3,400.

Of course, you'll never see bikers dealing drugs directly to users. They have intermediaries for that. It protects them from being caught, and when the person you're selling to has a financial stake in the operation, they are much less likely to rat on you to save their own skin. The closer you are to the final sale, the more vulnerable you are to being caught. That's why we bikers always let other people take the bigger risk.

That's where the girls come in. Shanna and Penny had been moving coke and Percodan tablets for Tom Craig for as long as I knew them. Once I was the guy with the coke, I started ferrying it from Tom to Shanna and Penny, and pocketing a huge amount of cash. Don't worry about poor Tom being cut out of the deal. Since I was buying from him, he didn't begrudge me taking my cut in exchange for him not having to take the stuff to Rooster's. I had to be careful, of course. Trevor was a friend and had a restaurant to run, and I never wanted him to get in trouble, so I never let him know what I was doing. Besides, Tom sold more stuff through Country BeBop's than I could ever move through Rooster's. It was no coincidence he called BeBop's his office.

So Shanna and Penny started working for me. I paid Tom for the ounces he supplied me, so he was happy. I made a profit when I sold them to the waitresses, so I was happy. Then they divided the ounces into gram and half-gram portions that they sold at a big markup to their customers, so they were happy. Hell, everyone was happy as far as I could see.

Deep down, I knew that it was no way to live, but it kind of made sense to me at the time, as long as I kept telling myself it was temporary. I just needed something to happen.

But what happened didn't change things the way I wanted. In the spring of 2000, my sponsor, Tom Craig, was diagnosed with a serious liver disorder. A few months after that, he was badly injured in a brutal motorcycle accident. His knee was fucked.

I felt bad, not just for Tom, but because I would miss riding around with him. With all the business and crime they read about, people forget that most guys join motorcycle clubs because they like riding motorcycles with other guys who also like riding motorcycles. I was one of those guys, and I would miss riding with Tom.

Like I said, Tom had been my sponsor. And when we patched over to the Hells Angels, I spent most of the day with him. He was quite the guy. Not tall or even that muscular, but he had a legendary reputation on the Danforth strip as a fighter. He had an Irish temper, and if you wanted to see it, you just had to tell him that, because he was fiercely proud of his Scottish heritage. But he was always a great guy, ready to help you out or have a laugh.

At least he was, until he changed. Back in the '80s, Tom was knifed in a bar fight. He later learned that the transfusion he had received during surgery contained some tainted blood. After he found out, the provincial government gave him a check for $10,000 for his inconvenience. The bad blood severely affected his liver, and by 2000, he was facing certain death if he did not receive a transplant right away. It did not take long before one became available, but he was never quite as healthy after that.

We were all happy to see Tom up and around after the surgery, of course, but he came out of the hospital a changed man. The leadership qualities, camaraderie and friendliness were gone. He'd always been hard on some people, but now, it seemed, he was that way with almost everyone. His wife, Sharon, became more of a nurse than a spouse. He was not as harsh with her as he was with many—because he depended on her so much—but his attitude toward her was not the way it had been before the operation. Tom had always been the kind of guy who could get other people to follow him and do what he wanted through his leadership prowess, but that left him after the surgery. The Tom we had known and respected now seemed to make bad deals and constantly push his luck—and his friends. Even if it was health-related, it was a hard change to watch. He was particularly hard on Bully.

I hadn't really articulated it to myself, but my life had changed to something I could hardly recognize anymore. Not long before, I had been happy and confident with my career in security, which seemed to be headed nowhere but up. I was spending my spare time riding and partying with my friends and having a great time. But by the time Tom had gotten out of the hospital, I had none of that left. The security career was gone—and I knew it was never coming back. I had a new job title, and I was not at all proud to say that it was "drug dealer." And riding with the guys who had been my friends became more of a chore than something I looked forward to. Hanging out with the guys was no longer what it used to be. It used to be all fun and games, getting drunk, fighting, fucking, having a great old time. It was the brotherhood I had been attracted to. But now it was all work.

I actually had to get drunk or high even just to tolerate them. The guys were all about money. And when Tom changed from a great guy, a true friend and real leader into a vicious and conniving loner who would abuse or cheat anyone he knew if there was an extra buck for him in it, it symbolized what we had all become.

I was a full-time biker. I woke up a Hells Angel, fell asleep a Hells Angel and spent every second in between as a Hells Angel. My duty was to serve the club. Sure, it had its perks, but it wasn't at all what I thought I had signed up for.

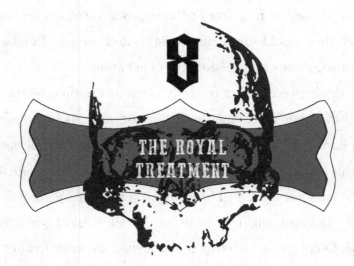

THE ROYAL TREATMENT

Being a Hells Angel is not like being a normal person. You get treated differently by everyone, and you get used to it pretty quickly. If I went to any bar in Scarborough, there would be no doubt that I was not going to wait in line, that there was always a great seat empty for me and that there would be a cool beer on the table before my butt hit the seat cushion. Of course, there was never any talk of me paying for anything. I couldn't have if I tried. My patch was like an entry pass for anything I wanted, a credit card I never had to pay off.

But not all the attention Hells Angels get is positive. My weekdays were spent rolling around Scarborough like some kind of nobleman visiting the village paupers in my domain. That's really what it felt like, because that's really how people treated me. Most people, that is. There was one group who saw the patch in another light. I was getting pulled over by the cops not only daily, but multiple times every day. I couldn't pass a Crown Victoria without its lights and siren going off. Every time they saw me, they felt it was their duty to stop me. Even if they were going in the opposite direction on the busiest street, they would throw on the lights and siren and pull a flying U-turn through any intersection just to get at me.

My driving record was perfectly clean at the time of the patchover, but that didn't last long. In fact, it got to the point where I had to work hard and pay a lot of money just to keep a valid license. I got bogus, shit-ass tickets almost every day. It seemed like they were making up traffic laws just to claim I broke them. I was even getting tickets in the mail—seriously, who ever heard of that shit? And I was hardly the only one. Every guy in the chapter was getting the same treatment.

It became a routine, almost like a kabuki. They stop you, tell you to take off your helmet and shut off the bike. Then they ask for your license and insurance. Once that checks out, they want to know where you're coming from and where you're going. You don't legally have to answer that, but you want to keep things as cordial as possible, so you tell them without too much detail. They always ask if you've had anything to drink, and you always, *always* say no, even if you have. It got to the point that, when I'd see the lights flash, I'd be at the side of the road, kickstand down, engine off, helmet off with my license and insurance in my hand before the cop was even out of his car. Still, you had to be careful not to reach into your vest pocket too quickly.

What we didn't know at the start, but later found out, was that the Ontario cops had been taking lessons from their compatriots in Quebec and B.C. on how to handle Hells Angels. And what they didn't know is that we had also been briefed by our friends in Quebec, and that we knew how to handle *them*. My papers were always in order, and I never carried anything sharper than a credit card or anything that shot faster than a sneeze. They could have stopped me a hundred times a day and never would have found shit.

Just because I knew how to handle the harassment doesn't mean I liked it. They weren't on to us; they were all over us. The police attention was so constant that if Bad Teri and I met after work for a drink, she would park in a different lot than I would, just to make it look like we weren't together. She'd been pulled over often enough to not want to be seen with me in public.

We knew they shared information on us, and we shared information on them. A lot of what we knew came from our regional meetings—they were later called presidents' meetings because the president of every chapter was required to attend.

Those meetings rotated from chapter to chapter, so when it was Toronto Downtown's turn, I was deeply involved. Prospects like me would rent cars, pick up the visiting members and take them to a prearranged, secure offsite venue. Normally, we were expected to disappear until we were needed to take the visitors back to their own cars, but sometimes we were required to stay to stand guard or go on coffee runs.

The guys inside the meeting were not allowed to leave until it was done, but they were well taken care of. One of our members, Phil, knew several high-end caterers, and he would order something like handmade pasta for the guys.

The meetings had agendas and minutes to be taken and distributed. Some Hells Angels, like Toronto Rob Chin Woo, were very computer-savvy and would collect, collate and email such documents to other clubs. It was all very corporate, like we were Labatt's or 7-Eleven or something. Nothing illegal was discussed, just club business. It's not illegal to be a Hells Angel, and we all wanted to keep it that way.

The club doesn't just take over your life, the club is your life. Being a Hells Angel is not like any other career, because there is no off switch. Even when you're not with the club, you're doing something related to the club. You're a Hells Angel 24/7, and the people close to you just have to put up with it.

Between the parties on weekends and my prospect responsibilities, there was precious little time for me to spend time with my girlfriend. We were living together, but in name only. I generally only saw her when we passed each other in the hallway. To be honest, she didn't really seem to care because she was into doing her own thing. Unfortunately, that meant a perc here, a glass a wine there and a gram of coke every couple of days.

We eventually broke up. As is commonplace with bikers who break up with their wives or girlfriends, I moved into the clubhouse. It wasn't a huge deal, it happens all the time and I was pretty popular among the guys, so I was welcomed there.

But, of course, I'd run into her pretty regularly at BeBop's, and without my realizing it, we were back on again. And then off again. Then on again until we were off again for good.

When it was clear to pretty much everyone that it wasn't going to work with us, a full patch named Carl Stoyan asked me if he could date her. It was one of those situations that was different in the biker world than it would have been with civilians. Instead of being apprehensive about it, I was honored. I mean, Stoyan was a full patch and I was just a prospect. And he was a real man's man, the kind of biker other bikers looked up to. He was never the type to bullshit anyone on anything.

Besides, I didn't have a choice. Stoyan was never a fan of mine—he didn't openly dislike me, but I could tell we just didn't quite mesh—and asking my permission was a mere formality. Since he was a full patch and I was a prospect, he was entitled, by club tradition, to take my girl even if we were still dating (and, in keeping with our biker culture, she would almost certainly not feel able to refuse). Bikers live by a different code when it comes to women. Lots of guys say stuff like "bros before hos," but it's mostly just posturing. In our world, though, bros came before everything (even, potentially, your life), and women were generally treated as property, with less importance than your colors, certainly, and, in some cases, your bike. It was different if you were married, though.

So it was with relief and a little bit of pride that I agreed.

At the time, my duties with the club were dedicated to support gear, mostly shirts and hats. I wasn't designing or ordering them, just making sure there were enough shirts at parties, so it was mostly about finding a place to stockpile merchandise and moving it to the clubhouse when necessary.

Luckily, one of the girls who was hustling at Rooster's, Shanna, was also housesitting for a customer she had gotten to know. So I kind of moved in with her there. I would store the support gear in the house and cut up ounces of coke into gram and half-gram packages in the kitchen.

The great thing about Shanna was that she was always under the radar. She drove a nice but conservative mid-sized car, she had looks I would describe as classy and she was impeccably well spoken. It made her something of a chameleon. She could talk to the club guys and communicate just as easily with teachers or parents.

We continued like that for months, all through the winter and into the spring of 2002. We looked like an ordinary Canadian family, except that the house wasn't ours and that we had a lot of cocaine going in and out.

We were living like that when the date for my membership vote came up. It certainly wasn't what I was picturing when I first got my Para-Dice Riders colors out of a closet in Tom Craig's basement.

As Stadnick had predicted, the Ontario members were slowly and painfully falling into what he called the Hells Angels way. We were being inundated with new rules, and, no matter how pica-yune, they all had to be followed to a T. Meetings with out-of-town members were commonplace, and every one of them resulted in a new set of regulations. Everyone, it seemed, was telling us what we had to change.

Of particular interest to the powers that be were our patches.

On the backs of our vests, there were four patches, and each was measured and examined to see if it complied with regulations. And all of them had to be the correct distance from one another.

In the center of the back is the crest, showing a skull wearing a Second World War aviator's helmet with wings. They're all the same, and they all come from the same company in Austria. Above that is the top rocker that says "Hells Angels" in red on white. Below the crest is the bottom rocker that indicates the region or territory its owner is in. Ours all said "Ontario." Stadnick had said that he wanted every

Canadian Hells Angel to wear "Canada" on their bottom rocker, but the separate regions hadn't quite gotten that close yet. The last patch on the back always says "MC" for "motorcycle club." By the time I was up for full-patch membership, I kind of scoffed at that. We were not a motorcycle club anymore. Riding was barely on our agenda. It certainly wasn't our focus. Making money was.

On the upper front left of the vest, over the owner's heart, there's usually a smaller version of the death's head crest. Below that is a small rocker that shows which chapter the owner belongs to. In Ontario, we had our guys in Downtown Toronto, as well as East Toronto, West Toronto, North Toronto, Woodbridge, Thunder Bay, Sudbury, Oshawa, Windsor, London, Kitchener, Hamilton and Ottawa.

Ottawa was different, though. The chapter was made up primarily of bilingual heavy hitters who had been through the biker wars in Quebec. Most of them had actually been on the other side during the war—members of the Rock Machine and Bandidos—including their president, Paul "Sasquatch" Porter. When they saw there was no way they could win the war, some of the top guys on the other side decided to turn their backs on their own clubs and join their sworn enemies, the Hells Angels. It always amazed me how easy it was for some bikers to ignore piles of bodies of their dead brothers when there was cash to be made from cocaine.

Because of their unique position, the Ottawa chapter was given the name Nomads. Years earlier, Stadnick had formed the original Nomads as a group of elite Hells Angels who didn't have a clubhouse because they were expected to be welcome everywhere. But when Porter and his buddies became the Ottawa chapter, that changed. They were known as the Nomads to indicate they were different from the rest of Ontario and just a cut above. They never went by the name Ottawa, always Nomads. And if you asked why, you'd be told that it was because Montreal said so.

They weren't the only ones with nicknames on their chapter rockers. For example, the guys from Hamilton wore the word *Hammer*, in part because the city's nickname is the Hammer, but also because they were reputed to like using hammers as weapons. Oshawa was known as the Asylum Crew because there was a mental hospital near their clubhouse. Our patches said "Downtown," even though our official name was just Toronto, because we didn't want to be confused with the chapters in west, east and north Toronto.

The right front of the vest is a little less regulated. It's a space that allows the owner to express himself a little bit. Two patches—a diamond-shaped 1-percenter and one that says "AFFA" (Angels Forever, Forever Angels)—are required, but the rest is up to the biker. Some patches are earned. There are dozens of them; for example, one that says "Filthy Few" indicates that the member has killed for the club, and one that says "Dequiallo" means the member has had a violent confrontation with law enforcement. Sometimes, a chapter will give its front rocker to a member of another chapter as a gift, an indication of respect. So if you see an Ontario Hells Angel with *Nomads* on the left and *Hammer* on the right, you know that he's part of the Ottawa chapter and that he has won the respect of the Hamilton chapter.

The patches are placed on a vest that's usually leather, but sometimes denim. It's funny to see the styles change over the years. These days, a lot of bikers are wearing Carhartt-style vests with quarter sleeves. The skateboarder style seems to be infiltrating their culture, and you'll see full-patch bikers with white tennis shoes, skinny jeans and skintight T-shirts, which seem to have replaced the tradition of functional jeans and jackets with any old shirt. But that's symptomatic of the wholesale changes in the biker world that I saw happen firsthand. When I started, it was all about slipping your colors and helmet on and riding. Those days are gone and are never coming back. You see a biker now, and he has a $100 Affliction T-shirt over his Versace denim. Fashion replaced function when the big money started rolling in.

Not every rule was about how we looked, though. Soon after the patch-over, the powers that be dropped another new rule on us: Before they could be put up for a membership vote, all prospects had to visit every other chapter in their region for a bar night.

That presented a major problem for me, even though I was not yet aware of the new rule. Tom Craig told me I was due at a church meeting in the first week of May. When I was waiting outside, as was customary, Tom came running out and, still panting, asked me if I had visited every chapter in Ontario yet. I told him that I had been to every single one except Thunder Bay. That shouldn't have surprised them too much. It's a hard seventeen-hour ride, and those guys have way more in common with the guys in Winnipeg than they did with us in Toronto.

He rolled his eyes and went back into the meeting. I was not invited in. When it broke up, TC came to me and told me I was going to Thunder Bay as soon as possible. He and Doug would pay my way.

So I went to Thunder Bay. I was still a prospect, so a bar night meant I was behind the bar, serving cocktails to the guests. A couple of lines of coke made that a lot easier. So did the guys. They were pretty hardcore, a bunch of old Satan's Choice members who seemed like they genuinely wanted to get to know me.

Later, we went to some bars, met some girls and had a lot of fun. Not a single member in Thunder Bay treated me with anything but respect and kindness. It's funny, but a lot of prospects treat visiting other chapters as a chore, like having to vacuum the house every Saturday. I didn't. I knew there would be work to do, but I've always worked and I didn't see what the big deal was. So when I visited Thunder Bay, I think they were surprised by my positive attitude and willingness to do what I had to do.

I do know that they certainly appreciated it when I came back to visit them once I was a full-patch member. Not even a year after I visited them the first time, I rode up there with boss John "Winner" Neal. We all rode out to Kenora and had a few drinks there. I could clearly tell that Winner was impressed by how many friends I had made in Thunder Bay.

Back in Toronto, I got to know Mary, Billy Dawson's wife. I don't know how they got together, because Billy had just come out of prison after a seven-year stretch. But, somehow, they were married.

Mary and I hit it off immediately. She was not big, but had a nice figure and eyes so full of life that they could almost put me into a trance. We had a strong connection, but it was never physical or romantic, just two people who sincerely liked each other. If anything, she was like a sister to me.

Mary was always a lot of fun, really quite mischievous, but also very responsible—her kids always came first. I mean, she could party all night long, but her kids always had nutritious lunches, clean clothes and finished homework for school every day.

It probably sounds crazy that Mary, who had so much going for her and was an excellent mother, would be married to a Hells Angel and spending her time partying all night with bikers, but there are reasons that things like that happen. Mary told me about how she had been brought up in a very unstable home and had experienced a very violent childhood. That's why she and so many other women and girls like her seek comfort among bikers.

Mary was a protector on an instinctive level, and not just of her kids. I remember this one short puke named Little Bill used to feel like he had carte blanche to hang around with us because his father was a friend of the club. He was one of those self-proclaimed tough guys who felt like they could take liberties with the club because we might say hi to him every once in a while or he might score a free drink when one of us would buy a round for the bar after a good day of gambling or selling stolen shit. But one day, he crossed the line. I'm not sure what he did to get her so riled up, but Mary took it upon herself to kick the living shit out of him. Of course, most men know not to hit a woman under any circumstances, and even a sniveling shit like Little Bill knew better than to defend himself against the wife of a full-patch Hells Angel. And Mary would be more than happy to point out that she was able to settle those kinds of matters. Normal people—citizens—might think about calling the cops if they saw that kind of thing, but we just thought it was hilarious.

Mary also served as my wingman with women sometimes. I remember bringing around one girl Mary just did not like. She would make funny faces behind the unsuspecting girl's back, trying—successfully—to make me laugh.

That's just the way it was with her. She loved to make fun of most of the people who tried to get too close or too friendly with anyone who was in the club. But she was quite discriminating. She just loved my dad—most people do—and when I introduced her to my wife to be, they got along immediately.

And, as protective as she was, she brought out the same instincts in me. For the longest time, I felt like she didn't belong where she was, doing what she was doing. I wanted to take her away from it all. But I would never get a chance.

Instead, I would spend my days in BeBop's. I'd see the owner—Bob "BeBop" Burton—there on a daily basis. He was a great guy, actually. Tall and in his fifties, he had gray hair and was as smooth as polished brass.

He was a tough guy from way back in the day, and he had made his money by running a very successful radiator repair shop. It was so successful, in fact, that it allowed him to buy a big house with a pool in the backyard in one of the nicest parts of Scarborough. We all found it at least a little bit funny that an ex–chief of police lived on the same block, because even though Burton was not in the club and wasn't a dealer, he had plenty of us as friends and we came by all the time.

Everybody loved BeBop, but he was best friends with Tom Craig. Tom had a cottage up north where he and BeBop would often go fishing. One weekend in the summer of 1998, he invited me, my buddy Jack and a couple of guys we all knew named Stan and Al up with them. Stan was a street-level dealer who made a fortune buying half-grams from us for $40 apiece and selling them to his civilian friends at a huge markup. Al was very much from Newfoundland. He was a pretty good mechanic and a swell guy to party with. A genuine family man, he was always a good guy to have around.

The trip was great, but it had a tragic ending. BeBop was driving back when he was involved in a collision. Stan died on the spot, Al was pretty fucked up and BeBop was really fucked up.

He had smashed both his legs, his hip bone, his ribcage and even his skull. After the accident, he had trouble walking for years. At one point, he could not handle stairs at all, and the washrooms were downstairs, so we set up a piss bucket for him at the bar. It was long-suffering Sheila's job to empty it from time to time. It didn't seem to bother her. Besides all of her work for Tom, she would tend bar, clean the place, run dope and generally make everyone feel welcome at BeBop's.

But she couldn't keep an eye on everything all the time. One day, we had been drinking for quite a while when a new waitress named Moira said she was going downstairs to get more ice. We didn't think much of it until we saw her come back up the stairs with Bebop's piss bucket full of ice. A bunch of us—BeBop, Doug Hoyle, Lorne Campbell and I—had been downing mixed drinks all day and immediately realized that it was not Moira's first time that day getting us ice. After a moment of shocked silence, BeBop spat his drink across the room. What could I do? I just told Moira that I was switching to straight vodka, no ice please. We laughed so fucking hard. Sheila educated her pretty fast after that.

Using the doctrine set out by Stadnick, Tom Craig always used citizens—straight-looking men and women who had nothing else to do with him or the club—to move his dope. One of them, of course, was Sheila. As I mentioned before, Tom treated her like shit, especially after his liver transplant. She sold his dope, she stashed his dope and his cash. She cleaned his house and she babysat his dog, Ace. Hell, she waited on both of them hand and foot.

I could never understand why her boyfriend let Tom treat her that way. The guy she was with was otherwise a pretty good dude. Bobby Prested was from Newfoundland and had been with Satan's Choice when they patched over to become Hells Angels East Toronto. An older guy, in his fifties, I guess he just thought it was good for business.

And that's how I spent my final days as a prospect. I'd show up at BeBop's every morning and shoot the shit with Sheila, who was always eager to get me caught up on all the gossip. We often did a line of coke to get things started, and we'd sit and chat with the usual crowd, the people who showed up with religious fervor to buy a half-gram and a perc. And they'd generally get them from Billy Campbell, the guy who sat in the corner of the bar, day in and day out from 10:30 to 5:30, like it was an office job. I can see him now. He was bald, stocky and had a cool pickup truck. I didn't really have much to do with him, though. He was TC's guy. That's what we'd say back then: "You can't sell to him, he's TC's guy." I had my own guys. But they were women.

9

FULL PATCH

So much had happened during my time as a prospect that it seemed like an entirely different life. I had quickly gotten used to the life—showing up at BeBop's, taking drugs, moving drugs and serving the full-patch members—that I almost forgot about becoming a member myself. *Almost*, of course, is the key word there. Although it wasn't at the front of my mind most of the time, I always knew that membership was my goal and could feel it deep down that it was the direction I was headed in.

I had leapt over the last hurdle the club had put in front of me. Like they'd told me to, I had visited the guys in Thunder Bay and won their respect. Because I had fulfilled all the requirements of membership, my picture was distributed to every Hells Angels chapter in the world. It's a test to see if anyone anywhere recognized me as a cop or someone who owed money on the street. The club uses it as a fail-safe method to uncover the identities of any infiltrators. Naturally, all I got were green lights.

I knew the vote for my membership was getting closer, so I was very upset when Magic asked me to be in two places at once. I knew that failing at either task would lead to discipline, which would lead to more prospect time. But I had no choice, so I took care of the one task that seemed more important, and—by necessity—let the other one slide.

When church night rolled around, it was warm, so I rode my bike to the clubhouse. That was one of the cool things about the Downtown chapter. We all had money. We all did okay, so we all rode some pretty good bikes. It wasn't that way at some of the out-of-town chapters. Some of those guys were so broke that if they didn't have a bunch of supporters, they'd be taking the bus to church.

As usual, the prospects were required to stay outside the actual meeting and stand guard. While I was at my post, a member came down and told me I was needed upstairs. I followed him into the room and was stunned by the silence. Every eye in the whole room was staring at me. Some of the guys looked sincerely pissed off, while the others were almost expressionless.

Now, I have spent my entire career assessing people. When I worked security, my primary instinct was to determine if someone was a friend or foe, and then I had to put everyone I came into contact with into an appropriate category. So as I walked into the room, I was mentally qualifying the look on each guy's face and calculating what kind of shit I was in.

Surrounded and the complete focus of every face in the room, I was asked why I wasn't able to complete both tasks I had been given.

I pointed out that they were both scheduled for the same time and aggressively replied, "Because there is only one of me."

Winner, the chapter president, told me to take my vest off.

Defiant, I told him I wouldn't. If they wanted a battle, I was in for a fight.

When I didn't take my vest off right away, Daryl Smith, the chapter's sergeant-at-arms and its toughest member, told me to take it off.

My response? "Fuck, no."

Doug Myles told me that I looked really pissed off. I told him that I guessed that I was.

Just as the tension was becoming unbearable, Winner stood up and said, "For fuck's sake, take that old vest off and put this new one on." He pointed to Dave Blackwood, who was carrying a full-patch member's vest custom-made for me. It was a Levi's denim vest with red shoulder patches that read "AFFA."

Immediately, everyone in the room leapt to their feet to hug me as I struggled to put my new colors on as quickly as I could.

What a moment. Magic, the guy who had always ridden me the hardest when I was a prospect, hugged me the longest. Terry Pink was kind enough to set me out a long line of coke.

And then, just as quickly as it had started, the celebration ended and it was back to business. I sat down and took my place among the other full-patch members. For them it was routine, but for me it was all new.

The next item on the agenda involved the Outlaws. The Outlaws were another 1-percenter club who ran the drug trade in large swaths of the American Midwest and chunks of Florida. Before the

Hells Angels moved into Ontario, they considered themselves big dogs there too, although the Mafia, based in Hamilton, refused to deal with them so they never had all that much product. They were supposed to be our rivals—the Hells Angels and Outlaws had fought several wars before, including a short but violent and one-sided one in Montreal when I was a teenager—but we didn't respect them much.

You have to see it the way we did. In a place like Ontario, lots and lots of guys want to be in motorcycle clubs, especially 1-percenter clubs. But very few of them has what it takes to get into a serious club, let alone the Hells Angels.

There was this guy we all knew named Jasper. He started hanging around TC when we were all still Para-Dice Riders, and he made it clear he was interested in joining. But as we got to know him, we all came to the consensus not just that he wasn't one of us, but he was actually little more than a waste of skin. He was way too old for the game, was a major bullshitter, a thief, a wife beater and, to top it all off, couldn't even get his bike to run.

Naturally, we showed him the door. And the next time we heard about him was when we found out he had become a full-patch Outlaw in less than a year. I even heard that his bike still didn't run.

While we didn't think very much of them, we certainly couldn't have the Outlaws disrespecting us in our own territory. That's how wars start. Apparently, the Outlaws were trying to move product in some Hells Angels bars in the west end of Toronto. And a couple of them had openly disrespected Mark Staples.

To be honest, I didn't know much about the Outlaws at all, nor did I know what Mark's business was. He was a brother, a friend and a guy who, I remembered, had changed his rockabilly hairstyle and sideburns to something more conservative when we patched over, but his business was his business. I would no sooner stick my nose in what he did than expect him to snoop around into what I was doing. That's how it works with 1-percenter clubs. It like what happened when the feds tried to bust up the Hells Angels south of the border. Sonny Barger admitted that there were plenty of criminals in the club—he even testified that he had sold heroin while he was a member—but they all worked individually or in small groups, never as a club. While he allowed that the Hells Angels was an organization full of criminals, it did not fit the U.S. government's own definition of a criminal organization. And that's the way we liked it. Every single member of a chapter might sell drugs, but since they did it individually and not as a chapter, it allowed us to stay a legal entity.

I did know that the Outlaws had a clubhouse on Nugget Avenue, an industrial backwater part of Scarborough, and that they hung out at strip joints.

Because the subject of the meeting was beginning to get sensitive, we knew we had to get out of the clubhouse. Anyone could be listening to us in there. So we got on our bikes and headed up to Magic's workshop up in Vaughan. It was my first time there, and I was surprised to see a shop that customized motorcycles could be so clean.

When we had all assembled, Winner took control of the meeting again. The Outlaws appeared to be trying to flex on our power in Toronto. If they were strengthening their numbers in Ontario, we had to be prepared. The first order that came down was that if we wanted to travel on our bikes, we had to have at least one other guy with us at all times. There was strength in numbers. We didn't want a war with the Outlaws, but if one came, we wanted to be prepared to win it.

When we decided we were ready for the Outlaws, we all rode back to the clubhouse, but there wasn't much to talk about, so we all went home. Well, I went to my buddy Conan's house and collapsed. I slept for a full day. It was one of the few times in my life I didn't get up early. It had been a long and sometimes shitty eight months, and the relief was sweet. It had been rough. I remember that one time when I slept on my friend Jack's couch, he actually had to have it steam-cleaned the next day because I was such a wreck that I made the couch smell unbearable.

By the time I woke up at Conan's, his kids had left for school and his girlfriend was already at work. So I proudly put my new colors on, got on my bike and headed for BeBop's. It was a short ride, but it took me more than an hour because I was pulled over twice.

I rode a lot that day and was stopped by cops every few miles in three different jurisdictions.

It's always the same old routine at traffic stops—produce your paperwork, tell them where you were headed and where you were coming from—but different cops have different styles. Some try to be your buddy. It's usually the older ones who've been through it a million times, just like you have. They want to get you talking—maybe you'll spill something you shouldn't have. You have to be careful with those guys. Some other cops are nervous, even a little bit scared. But the worst are the guys who are actually scared, because they always put on the tough-guy act. They'll try to provoke you into doing something stupid. I'd never fall for it. No matter who stopped me, I tried to be friendly and polite, but non-engaging. My idea was to give them as little as I could get away with legally, and smile the whole time.

The plainclothes dedicated biker cops were way better to deal with than the old harness bulls. They were familiar with the life and knew most everybody in it. That made them easier to get along with because they could relate. And they could even be useful. When TC was in an accident (he'd had a few), he'd always tell the uniformed cop to call the BEU because he knew they could get in touch with his wife or BeBop right away. Even the great Walter Stadnick asked a Hamilton biker cop to protect him when he was in a hospital, recovering from an accident, and was sure the Mafia or the Outlaws were out to kill him.

At the time, there were cops everywhere, like a cloud of wasps, all out to get us. And it wasn't just the harness bulls stopping our bikes and cruising by at low speeds. We saw guys—obviously cops—with the same faces and same cars day in and day out. It seemed like every anti-biker cop in the world was watching us.

I had learned methods of burning a tail—or even a whole surveillance team—during my security career. I had told WR that I would never reveal them, but I broke that promise with the other guys in my chapter. I figured that if one was caught, it would greatly increase the likelihood that we were all going to get caught, so it seemed like a necessary move at the time.

Of course, the biker cops were different than regular cops. I would later learn how similar they were to us. They saw the similarity, but we didn't.

I had my first experience with a biker cop when Tuck and I were running out to get pop, chips and strippers for a Para-Dice Riders party. OPP detective George Cousens and his partner, Greg Swiss, came over to our car, as friendly as if they'd known us for years.

I'd later get to know George quite well. One time, when my mother was undergoing chemo, he stopped me while I was driving her car. He asked me who the car belonged to, so I told him the whole story. George seemed genuinely moved by my mom's struggle with cancer and told me that he hoped she'd pull through. Maybe he was just cultivating a source, but it seemed like he really cared.

I'd most often see George at the roadblocks they set up outside our parties. One time we were headed up to a Satan's Choice party in Port Perry, and he stopped me along the way. There was an OPP helicopter hovering over the party site, and I asked him if he'd flown in one. "Yeah, a few times," he told me. "It's not a big deal." I had to disagree, and told him I thought it would be pretty cool. He smiled and admitted, "Yeah, it's pretty cool."

Once at the clubhouse, I showered and ate some boiled eggs, chased down with a couple of beers. The place was quiet, in large part because we hadn't started doing twenty-four-hour security yet.

It was the early summer in Toronto. Since there was nothing going on at the clubhouse, I got back on my bike and rode over to Doug Myles's house. He seemed pretty happy that I was now a full-patch member, but we took a few minutes out to reminisce about the time when I was a striker.

He told me that he was surprised it had taken me as long as it had to become a member. He pointed out that Jason Tuck, who started the same day as me, got his patch in just six months. But things were different for me. There wasn't just the Thunder Bay fiasco; I also had to take some time off due to illness—nothing that serious, just keeping up the family tradition of spotty health. And to top it all off, my mom was dying of cancer.

It was just what I needed. Over more beer, Dougie and I had a nice, relaxing conversation. His wife was there too. I always liked her.

And what Doug said to me had stuck in my head. He told me that, as a full-patch member of the Hells Angels, I could do anything I wanted. I could travel the world, stay at any clubhouse, party all I wanted, get any amount of dope I wanted and all the women I could handle. But he warned me not to let it go to my head. He told me that civilian laws were no big deal—there was always a way around them—but that I had to be very careful not to break the club's rules. If I followed them, he said, life would be easy and immensely rewarding. If I broke them, I would be fucked. And on my own.

After Doug's, I rode up to Magic's house in Vaughan. He had an awesome place, very neat and well kept and decorated with tons of photos, many of them from when he was in a club called the Foundation MC.

I was never all that close to Magic, but I knew that he was a heavy hitter with an impressive network of friends. One time when I was still doing personal protection, he asked me to find him a bullet-resistant car. The funny thing was, I just happened to have access to one. I was actually trying to sell it on behalf of a client who had to leave the area as fast as he could. I invited Magic to look at it, but when he saw it, it looked like shit because it was in the middle of being detailed, so he passed.

Just like Doug, he spoke to me about the difference between being a prospect and a full-patch member. He told me that all the guys liked me and admired the work I had done, but the consensus was that none of them thought I was a natural criminal. I admired his honesty, so I told him point-blank that I wasn't a criminal by trade or by choice. It was just how the cards had fallen. He laughed and said he understood. Then he told me, "Ya gotta survive, Davey."

Before I left, he stopped me and told me he had something for me. It was a sweater he had picked up while visiting another chapter. That's one of the things that happens when you get your patch: people start giving you gifts. Hell, BeBop actually bought the vest I was wearing and Dave Blackwood sewed on all the patches. The only one who did not get me anything was TC. Hell, he didn't even acknowledge my new status for a very long time.

The usual crowd was waiting for me at BeBop's, and they were ready to celebrate. To my utter delight, there were drinks and lines of coke, all free. I could get used to this, I thought to myself.

Sheila was working and dropped by to say congratulations. But I could sense some concern in her voice. She told me I should get out of the life, said I was too good for it. I thought that was funny—I mean, considering her deep involvement in TC's drug trafficking operation. She suggested I find a nice girl and move away, do something else with my life and be happy. I told her I'd think about it.

I spent the whole day there, drinking. After BeBop's closed, I was pretty wasted and had no desire to be stopped by the cops again, so I took a cab to the clubhouse. There were a few members already there, partying. Terry Pink was there, and so were Lou and Psycho Dave. Seeing them having a good time and knowing that I didn't have to serve anyone anymore kind of gave me a second wind, so I grabbed a drink and joined in.

Before too long, Daryl Smith joined us. Daryl and Psycho Dave played together in a metal band called Brass Knuckle Therapy. I really liked them, in no small part because they could play anything from Elvis and Merle Haggard to Iron Maiden and Motörhead equally well.

As the party lingered into the early-morning hours, all that remained were Daryl, a couple of his friends and me. One of his friends just happened to be a statuesque beauty named Tracey. She was built like a Playboy bunny and had cute freckles, and she could not keep her eyes off me.

I was talking to a prospect named Guy when Daryl came over to tell me he had some blow at his apartment and that Tracey had told him she wanted to get to know me better. Besides, he said, the sun was already up and it would be wise to move our little party to a quieter place. I didn't need to be told twice.

As it turned out, Tracey and I ended up spending several days together. She even met my dad and attended my mom's funeral (along with the whole club and lots of police). She got along with Sheila, but I knew it wasn't meant to be when I found out that Mary disapproved of her. Besides, Tracey had a pretty high-octane job at an executive headhunting company, and if the cops ever showed up there, she would almost certainly be fired. We decided it would be best for everyone if Tracey moved on.

While it wasn't as structured as my security career, I had settled into a routine. It consisted mainly of riding from bar to bar in Scarborough. I'd hang out at BeBop's, mostly with Sheila, and then deliver coke from Tom to Rooster's, where the girls would sell it and I would party every night.

One time when I got to Rooster's, I could see that Billy Dawson was inside. As I was walking in, his wife stood up and ran over to the door, blocking my way. She said that Billy had a court order that stipulated he was to have no association with any club members or anyone with a criminal record. She told me to give Billy half an hour to do some business, pay his bill and get out. Of course, I didn't want to see him go back to jail over nothing, so I went across the street to some bar and hung out there by the window. About forty minutes later, I saw Billy and his wife leave Rooster's, so I walked over. Right there, out in the street, Billy came over and hugged me. So much for not associating with Hells Angels.

But he had his reasons. Not only was it the first time he'd seen me since I earned my patch, but I was working for him and doing a good job. The fact was that we saw each other all the time, just not out in public like that. Billy was giving me $1,700 for every kilo of coke that I carried just a few blocks for him. Compare that to the $100 per kilo TC was giving me. But Billy was different than TC. He was a career drug dealer, and a good one. He knew how to get and keep customers and people to work for him.

Things got more than a little mixed up when Billy went to jail, though. When Billy went down, Martin C, who had been buying off Billy for years, naturally turned to TC for product. Of course, when

Billy got out, he wanted Martin C's business back. Most people would think it would be easy enough for Billy and TC to work out a plan that served both their interests—maybe a merger of sorts—so that they could both profit. But that's not how Hells Angels work. Instead, Billy beat the crap out of Martin C for being disloyal and buying from TC. And then TC beat him up for going back to Billy. Billy and TC never had a problem with each other over the whole thing, just with poor Martin C.

There was a big difference between Billy and TC when it came to coke. Billy was getting his from Henry, and it was pretty decent. But TC was getting his from Quebec, and it was primo stuff. Just for laughs, I had bought a coke purity tester from Spy Depot on Yonge Street, which was co-owned by an old friend of mine, and tested them both. Billy's cocaine usually ran about 50 percent pure, while TC's always scored in the high 80s.

I had another job, and that was to ferry cash from Billy to Henry. It was always either $18,000 or $35,000 for a half-kilo or a kilo and, without fail, wrapped in a paper bag from KFC. Every time I dropped a bag off, I told Henry to count it, but he never did. So you can imagine how pissed off I was when the little crook started telling people one of the packages was short. Billy told him, "There's no way Davey would have dipped in." TC also took my side, in part because he was with me when Billy handed me the bag, he watched me count it in the back room of Rooster's, and he rode with me to the clubhouse. He even watched me put the bag in Henry's hands.

I would later learn that Henry had a long and storied history of trying to pull off that same kind of rip. It was well known that if he hadn't had family pull in the club, Henry would have been kicked out of it long ago and might even have been nothing more than a brief stop on our annual graveyard run (when we visit the burial sites of deceased members) every fall.

Because the cops are so obsessed with it, the process for distributing cocaine is precise and complicated. My primary contact was Billy's runner, Patrick "Red" Fox. He was a good guy in his early twenties. I remember him once, happily chatting with my girlfriend's mom for hours. My mom loved him too; he was just that kind of guy.

I would meet with Billy at Rooster's, and he would tell me what he needed. It was usually something like three kilos. I would then meet up with Patrick at the clubhouse and whisper something like "Hey, our guy in the East End needs . . ." and then I'd hold up three fingers. He'd relay the message to Henry, who would reply within twenty-four hours with a time and place for the drop-off.

Because of the attention it drew from law enforcement, I wouldn't ride my bike when I was carrying cash or coke. I would rent a car or even take public transit to get to the rendezvous point. It was always a strip mall. I would always arrive early and wait in the car until I saw Red. He would not acknowledge me, but would walk into a store—it would usually be someplace big enough to have unchecked corners, but not so busy that someone would notice the drop-off—and I would follow him inside.

He would place the coke somewhere inconspicuous, and I would pick it up later. There was never any hand-to-hand contact or any public interaction that indicated that we knew each other. That's what's called a dead drop. If the cops grabbed me with the coke in my possession, I could always say that I had found the package in the store and was trying to get it back to its owner. I would tell them I hadn't even looked inside to see what it was. I was just doing my part to be a good citizen.

Once I had the coke, I'd head over to Mike Stern's place in Scarborough's Morningside neighborhood. I would call Shanna, who would then call Mike to let him know I was coming. Mike rented two apartments in the same high-rise. One was for him and his girlfriend, and the other was for the coke. He had given me a key to the building, so I would park around back and let myself in. Then I would run up the stairs—because I would be trapped in a box with strangers, I'd never use the elevator—for the most exercise I got all week, and drop the package off with Mike.

The only things I had to worry about would be if Red had been followed or if Mike's building was under surveillance. If either of those things ever happened, I'd get arrested, but I was pretty sure a smart lawyer would be able to talk my way out of any major trouble, claiming my ignorance if not exactly innocence.

Once the coke was in Mike's hands in Morningside, I'd drop off the rental car and make my way to a bar, where I'd see Billy in the back room. We had to be super careful so that nobody, including Trevor, knew what we were doing in there. Then Mike would pay me. At $1,700 a kilo, I'd make $5,100 cash just for taking a small package from a store to an apartment.

TC's operation was a lot simpler and a lot less profitable for me. I'd show up at BeBop's and TC would hand me a package. He'd then say something like "Here, take this Christmas present over to the barber shop on Eglinton." I'd drive or ride the subway over to the place and drop off the package. When I came back, TC would hand me $100 for every kilo I had carried over.

It was actually a pretty okay life except for one thing—Tom. He was getting steadily worse, treating everyone—Sheila, me, members and supporters—like shit. He couldn't party after the transplant, so he called everyone with a beer an alcoholic and everyone who bought coke from him a drug addict. It bothered me that he couldn't see the irony in that, since he was a big-time dealer and used to get as drunk and high as anyone before the doctors told him he couldn't. What a fucking hypocrite.

But don't get the idea that all I did was move drugs around. I was at a barbecue once with a few friends, and a woman approached me, asking me what I did for a living. Before I could answer, my buddy Hank stepped in and told her all about my career in security.

She told me that she worked for a private finance company that held the papers on tons of leased restaurant, dry cleaning and party equipment. She also explained that several of the clients involved had gotten far behind in their payments and that getting the stuff back was not easy. Restaurant equipment isn't like a car, which can be towed or even driven away whenever the debtor isn't in it. When you go to repossess a deep fryer, it's almost certainly in use and full of hot oil. Moving it is not easy. And the only way to get to it is to confront the person who's using it, whose livelihood almost certainly depends on it, and they will not want to give it up easily.

After we all got comfortable after some drinks and food, she asked me if I'd like to work for her. I was more than happy to get some legitimate work. And I didn't even have to lift anything. All I had to do was get the debtors to pay or take the equipment back. I actually thought that my primary purpose would be to make sure nobody messed with the crews she assigned to pick the stuff up. It seemed so easy that it should have been illegal.

On the following Monday, I showed up at her office, dressed in my best golf shirt, pressed trousers and dress shoes, for an interview. I nailed it and started working on her delinquent cases right away.

The first few weeks were kind of boring. I would talk to the delinquent cases, and the debtors knew that if they made a partial payment, even a promise, on their outstanding debt, it would get us off their backs, at least temporarily. But I wasn't interested in that. I wanted full payment, with interest.

I started visiting them. There was this one fresh pasta–making restaurant up in Vaughan. On the phone, the guy cried poverty, saying that business was slow and his rent was too high. So I showed up. For five consecutive days, I sat in his parking lot, watching hordes of customers go in and out. Eventually, I went in, looked around and lingered over an espresso while watching his business run. That made it fairly simple to estimate his average sale and number of customers per day, and then extrapolate to guess his total revenue.

Then I called his landlord. You can't just ask how much someone is paying, so I posed as a dry cleaner looking for a similar location of about the same size and on the same street.

It was hardly an exact science, but it did give me a decent estimate of how much he actually had coming in and going out. And it gave me a piece of paper to refer to when I brought it up.

So I waited until Tuesday morning, which I knew was the restaurant's least busy time period, to drop by and ask to speak with the owner. Yeah, it was an Italian place in Vaughan, but I didn't worry about this guy being mobbed up, because there's no way a connected guy would be leasing his equipment from some Mickey Mouse outfit like ours in Newmarket.

When he came out, I introduced myself, handed him my business card and told him he had to address his outstanding debt. He invited me to discuss it over espresso with lemon wedges. With a great deal of passion and drama, he claimed poverty again.

So I pulled out my papers with my estimates of his revenue and costs. He was astonished. I told him I didn't even count the high school kids who came in and bought one little thing or the one-offs who showed up from time to time. Just his regular customers.

He couldn't argue, because his own books said basically the same thing. He was caught dead to rights and I knew it was time for the restaurant owner to play his one and only trump card. He pulled a business card out of his wallet. The name on it was Gord and it said he belonged to the Last Chance MC. That's when I realized where his cash was going. Gord had this guy paying protection. If you don't already know, protection is one of the oldest rackets in the organized crime books. What happens is that some tough guy—in this case, a biker named Gord—offers to protect the restaurant from vandalism, harassment and robbery in exchange for a regular payment. But the tacit agreement is that if the money is not paid, the person offering the protection is actually the one to worry about. To understand it better, consider a scenario in which you bought an auto insurance policy under which your insurance agent would smash your windshield with a sledgehammer if you missed a payment.

Of course, I knew Gord. Last Chance had patched over at the same time as the Para-Dice Riders and had become the Hells Angels West Toronto chapter. So it was easy for me to arrange to meet Gord and the owner the following day. It was delicate business, though, and I had to be very cautious because of the club's intricate rules about rips involving other brothers.

I was more than a little surprised when Gord refused to agree to meet with me beforehand to make a mutually beneficial arrangement to have when we talked to the restaurant owner. But when I saw him, it made more sense. Gord had been a boxer, but those days were a distant memory. He was old now, with a big gut, and he looked like he needed every penny he was squeezing out of this guy. At the meeting, he wouldn't budge.

I knew smoking a full-patch like Gord wasn't going to happen (not only would there be hell to pay from the club if I beat him up, but I knew it would make the restaurant owner think I was nothing more than a common thug), so I decided to deal with it in the way I had seen the high-powered executives I used to protect do it. I thanked Gord for his time and, in front of the restaurant owner, told him to fuck off. This is between us, I told him, and I would deal with the debtor later.

I could tell that Gord was uneasy. I don't think he had ever been spoken to like that before. Smart bikers know to stay within their limits. Gord had been a big fish in a small pond for years and gotten used to it. But now there was a bigger fish in his pond, me, and he was going to have to deal with that or find another pond. Fuck club brotherhood, this was business.

I let the restaurant owner know that I was also a Hells Angel. But I was from Downtown Toronto and Gord was from West Toronto. It's not the same; they're not as strong. That was enough. We worked out a payment structure that allowed the debt to be cleared in full. What happened to Gord's cut? I don't know, and I don't care.

After that, I asked the restaurant owner for his front door key. He produced it and I went and copied it. I came back and gave him his original. He was so nervous, he accidentally left it on the table when he went back to work.

I wasn't totally convinced that this guy (or Gord) was 100 percent trustworthy enough to keep his word, so I let myself into the restaurant after closing and placed my business card on every oven and bread maker that he was leasing from the company.

He paid. He came up with $15,000, which made my cut $4,000. Not bad when you consider it was all legal and there was no violence involved. The leasing company had no idea how I collected the debt. They were just glad I did.

I told my sponsors what had happened, in part because I wanted to know if there would be any blowback from West Toronto because of my dealings with Gord. They laughed and said I should have belted them both and brought back some pasta. They were so impressed by my creative method of getting a deadbeat to pay that they tried it out themselves.

As busy as I was, I found myself spending most of my time with Sheila, which was actually really enjoyable when Tom wasn't around.

One day, she asked me for some pot. That surprised me, but I wasn't really too suspicious because I trusted Sheila. I had never sold pot, but I knew where I could get some because I knew somebody who had ripped off a ton of pot from a grower who worked for another club. So I agreed to get her some.

What happened next should have tipped me off, and it probably would have if it had been anybody other than Sheila. When I arrived with the weed, she just took what I handed her and gave me the money. She didn't even look in the bag. It's not just that she trusted that the pot would be in there, but I knew that pot buyers are the pickiest, most precise people in the world. Pot growing and preparation (even smoking) these days have evolved into art forms, and buyers always, always, always check out the product for smell, moisture, impurities and other traits. For them, everything has to be just right or they will complain or even haggle. When she didn't bother to look, just grabbed it and tucked it away, I was surprised, but not quite suspicious.

Then she asked me for some percs. That really surprised me. I mean, lots of people in BeBop's sold percs, and I was not one of them. Besides, Tom had a major perc-moving operation in that area, and she stashed his shit at her apartment anyway. I knew she'd never steal from Tom, but wouldn't it be easier, I thought, just to ask him? And wouldn't she get a lower price from him? I told her I had no idea where I could get the hundred percs she had asked for at a low enough price so that both she and I could turn a profit. In fact, I told her, I would probably end up getting them from Tom.

She convinced me that she couldn't go to Tom because he was acting like such a prick to her, accusing her of being an addict and only being out for herself. I believed her. He had become annoyingly judgmental. She told me that she didn't want to deal with him any more than was absolutely necessary. She even went so far as to tell me that it would be better if Tom didn't know she was buying any. I reluctantly told her I would hook her up.

At the same time, she was constantly telling me to leave the club, stop dealing drugs and go clean. They weren't just mixed messages; they were falling on deaf ears. The club had become a huge part of my life. In the winter of 2002, I had my hands full, driving from bar to bar to keep an eye on my little empire as well as keeping up my social duties with the club. I knew I was feeling a lot of stress because I was packing on the pounds. I've always been a big guy, but by that time, I was huge, maybe 380 pounds at my peak.

Travel was a major part of it. Not long after Sheila asked for the percs, I had to go to a funeral in Edmonton and, soon after that, another one in B.C. There were parties, but they were never that much fun. We'd get some much-needed relief whenever Quebec would throw a party. They were first-class events in which they would reserve an entire floor of a hotel. All the doors to every room were open and they were full of dancing girls, all the booze you could imagine and lines of coke on every flat surface.

It would get pretty unreal because guys would do whatever they felt like, right out in the open. Like one time, Doug Myles and I came across one of our guys in a hallway while he was enjoying a stripper—and pleasuring himself at the same time. I can tell you that it made us both pretty uncomfortable, but there wasn't much we could do. The guy in question was a well-respected member who had done time for the club. I particularly admired how he was eager to recapture some of the old riding and partying brother-hood we had essentially lost after the patch-over. So who was I to judge him?

When spring came, all I could think about was riding. It was almost riding weather when a guy walked into BeBop's and said he was a member from Quebec called Sky. We knew that there was a member from Quebec named Sky—he had even been national president at one point—but we couldn't be sure this guy was him. The real Sky, we knew, had fled from the cops to Morocco after the Sherbrooke Massacre, and had been arrested years later, almost by accident, when a vacationing biker cop ran into him in line to buy lottery tickets at a resort-town convenience store. Sure, the real Sky would be welcome, but how could we be sure it was him? Back then, there were no smartphones that could send a photo to Montreal for verification.

Something didn't seem right about the guy to me. After a while, I told him, "No disrespect, pal, but I don't believe you."

We called in a couple of veteran Para-Dice Riders who might be able to shed a little light on the situation. By the time Lorne Brown from the Woodbridge chapter and Dougie Myles showed up, TC and I had already decided the guy was a liar and we really wanted to crush him. When we said that, Doug told us to hold on. He listened to what the guy had to say, and enough of it jibed with what he knew that he wasn't sure if this was the real Sky or not. So Tom and I stood down. But I have to admit, I kind of enjoyed the excitement of an impending beatdown. It reminded me of the good old days.

Frustrated, the guy claiming to be Sky left, and three other guys—who said they were friends of his—walked in. One of them started shooting off his mouth and acting like he owned the place, even doing lines of coke right off a table.

I couldn't help but laugh. TC wasn't in as charitable a mood and he told the guy off. I don't know why, maybe the cocaine gave the guy some courage, but he told TC to fuck off and called him a fat bastard. It was then that he gave the word. "Shaky," he said. "Kill him."

Tom threw one of the guys over a few chairs, and I knocked another out with a single punch. That put me nose to nose with the mouthpiece. For a moment, I thought that we might be being set up. I wondered to myself if these guys could have been sent in by some other club or the cops to see what really happened inside BeBop's, our closely guarded inner sanctum.

That moment of hesitation gave Mouthpiece a chance to escape. He ran to the door and even made it into his Chevy Blazer. Desperate, he slammed it into reverse and stomped on the accelerator. The big vehicle flew over the parking barriers and sidewalk right into the traffic of Kennedy Road.

Even with his head start and all the extra weight I was carrying at the time, I managed to grab the passenger door and open it. In his panic, the open door hit a telephone pole, leaving behind a puddle of shattered glass. That was the last we saw of Mouthpiece, as he sped down Kennedy alone with his destroyed passenger door hanging off.

Back inside, some of the guys were having a little fun with the two assholes Mouthpiece had left behind. They later walked back to wherever it was they had come from, but I don't think it was easy for them.

Later, I found out that the guy who claimed to be Sky wasn't. But he had shared a cell with him, so he knew everything about him. He also knew that a former national president would have all the booze, coke and women he could ever want, so he thought he'd take his shot. The other guys? Along for the ride.

It wasn't long after that that Sheila reminded me I hadn't yet gotten her the hundred percs she had asked for. Again, I was mystified. There was no shortage of the little white fuckers in her life. Hell, she was friends with a couple named Trent and Monica who sold them right out of their house. Or she could just ask Billy Campbell, who sold all day every day in BeBop's while she got him beer after beer. He was mainly a coke dealer, but everyone knew he could get percs too.

I simply couldn't understand why she wanted them from me. I figured she must not have done the math. I sure had. Percs retail on the street for $5 a pill. So a hundred would be worth $500 if they sold a pill at a time, which would be a pretty painstaking and time-consuming process. Plenty of people bought in bulk, and the going rate was $4 a pill if you bought five or more at once. Even if I somehow managed to acquire them for $350 (and that would be a stretch), there would only be an absolute maximum of $150 to split between us. It wasn't worth the time and effort, let alone the risk.

She was insistent, and I really liked her, so I looked into it. None of the perc dealers I knew would sell to me for less than retail, so they were out. I didn't want to go to Tom because Sheila had asked me not to and, frankly, I knew he'd be an asshole about the whole thing.

I did know a guy, my old buddy Grant. He wasn't a club guy. In fact, he wasn't aligned with anyone. Just a guy who bought and sold things, including drugs. I knew him from the Falcon's Nest. I thought he was okay, a tough guy with a winning sense of humor, but for some reason, the other guys in the club did not like him.

Grant actually had a legitimate prescription for Percodan, but he didn't use them. He had gone through all kinds of rehab programs, like Alcoholics Anonymous, and was quick to tell anyone other than a doctor with a prescription pad that he was two years sober. Meant fuck all to me, but it made him proud. And a guy who had lots of percs to sell.

So I had ol' Grant pay me a visit at BeBop's. Sure, he had some percs to sell, he told me. And since we were old friends, he would let me have a hundred for $350. I promised Sheila she could have them for $400, so I went to all that concern and trouble for a lousy $50. Look at me, I'm Pablo Fuckin' Escobar.

I knew I was being followed by Biker Enforcement Unit officers. I always was, but it seemed much more conspicuous all of a sudden. I distinctly remember telling TC that I had seen two or three guys who always seemed to be in strategic spots to watch me, no matter where I went. He told me to get over it, that I was just being paranoid.

When I was leaving, a guy named Benny told me he'd seen one cop-looking dude climb into the backseat of his car, and it looked like he was still there. I told Benny he'd done a good job and I fucked off through the back door of BeBop's on my way to the clubhouse.

As I had been both a top security guard and a Hells Angel, I thought strategically. I took only side streets and varied my speeds, doubling back every once in a while. I saw the same two cars at three different points along the way. There was no way that would have happened if they weren't following me.

I made a U-turn and stopped. I immediately noticed that the cars were doing a standard grid-type holding pattern that we had all been taught. So I waited, leaning on my bike with my helmet off until they disappeared. It was only then that I rode to the clubhouse.

The second I got there, I told Doug and TC that it seemed to me that the attention I was receiving from law enforcement had noticeably increased. They scoffed and said it was normal. But I knew it was far from normal.

I mentioned it to Rob Chin Woo. He explained that the cops only have so much time and a limited budget, so they will focus on newer members to see what they bring to the club. According to him, the cops were undermanned and underfunded and had their work cut out for them. The Hells Angels were a huge organization, and the cops had to look for weak links if they were ever going to be able to make any kind of case against the club. My job, he told me, was to not be a weak link.

After talking to him, I was relieved on an intellectual level, but couldn't shake the gut feeling that something just wasn't right.

I tried to get back to normal. For me, that meant traveling. I had a toothbrush at my dad's, at my girlfriend's and at the clubhouse. I also had regular meetings with Doug Hoyle, Carson Mitton, Keith Gallagher, Bobby Prested and Bernie Walczak about club schedules and other administrative business. And I was still moving coke for TC. I was up to whole kilos, which he would get from Montreal's

Irish mafia, better known as the West End Gang. They would show up at BeBop's and go into a corner with TC for a private meeting. They looked nothing like gangsters, just a bunch of average Joes.

And everywhere I went, the same Buick LeSabre kept turning up.

At the end of March 2003, things began to change. I was used to seeing cops, but suddenly they were everywhere. There were cops at every place I went—tons of them at my dad's, at my girlfriend's, at the bars I went to every day. But at the same time, the traffic stops just stopped happening. I would ride past cop cars, and all they would do is watch me go by. For someone used to being stopped five or six times a day, I can tell you it was very unnerving, to say the least.

I told TC and Doug what was going on with the cops, and they both dismissed it as my paranoia. TC had gotten so incredibly greedy that he couldn't see anything but money. The very idea that something could put his gravy train in jeopardy was not something he seemed to be able to comprehend. And Doug? Well, he just didn't care. He kept his shit tight. When it came to his personal business, nobody knew anything about what Doug was doing. He sincerely believed he had fuck all to worry about.

It was during that period that there was one truly beautiful night. The weather was so great that Conan and I brought some girls to my dad's house to enjoy a few pops by the pool. It was just starting to get dark when we pulled up and saw my dad and his new (and eventually long-term) girlfriend headed out for a night on the town. We tried to talk them into a drink or two, but they had plans.

Just as we were getting off our bikes, a Ford Taurus with two guys in suits passed by very slowly. It could not have been more obviously an unmarked police car. It was the feds. They were passing by so slowly, almost idling, on an otherwise quiet suburban side street. It was like they weren't even trying to pretend they weren't cops.

It was just so ridiculous that we started laughing at them. Feeling pretty cocky, I yelled, "Hey, Fuck-o, you're on a dead-end street," to let them know how stupid it was to think we hadn't made them. "You want a beer?" I shouted. "You're burned; you must be thirsty."

The cop in the passenger seat gave me the finger.

Conan was upset. He told me he didn't need any heat because he was on the last few points on his license and could not afford to lose it. He was always concerned about cops. He was a strong family man, a great dad, and he was careful not to endanger his family.

We had another guy with us, Stevie D from the Vagabonds MC. As a Vagabond, he wasn't supposed to hang out with Hells Angels like me, but we figured that since we weren't doing any business together, it was okay. He was worried too. He told me that if I wasn't getting stopped anymore, and if the feds were watching my dad's house 24/7, they were gathering intel to use against me.

Ah, phooey, I thought, and we spent the night drinking by the pool until the sun came up, about the time my dad came home. We started busting his balls about being out all night. It wasn't very responsible, Conan told him. My dad had a cup of Tim Hortons coffee in his hand and said, "Fuck off, Steve" (using Conan's real name) and started to get ready to go to work. My dad never liked the club or me being in it, but he did love having the guys over. And a guy like Conan—who wasn't in the club—was always welcome to have a few beers.

* * *

On April 4, 2007, my girlfriend was at her place way out in the west end, but I was too tired to make the ride. Instead, I went to my dad's place. I frequently dropped by to check on him after Mom died. Besides, Bully, TC, BeBop and a few other guys had invited me to go fishing with them that weekend and I wanted to borrow my dad's fly rod.

At 5:45 that morning, the Toronto police's ETF (it stands for Emergency Task Force, but they call themselves "Extra Tough Fuckers") smashed his front door down and arrested me. I was on my feet by the time they came in the door. The familiar squeak of the side gate had gotten me up.

"Hands up!" they shouted. "Who's here?"

They were fully armored for battle and armed to the teeth. There was just one biker and an old man in the house, but they weren't taking any chances. I was, after all, sergeant-at-arms of the Toronto chapter of the Hells Angels.

10

BEHIND BARS

For a Hells Angel, getting arrested is not like it is for a civilian. For one thing, if you're in the club, you kind of expect it to happen. Everybody told me I'd be arrested eventually. Maybe I didn't really think it would happen to me, but I have to admit I wasn't totally surprised when it did.

When a civilian gets arrested, they have all kinds of thoughts running through their heads. "What am I gonna tell my boss?" "What am I gonna tell my family?" It's different for Hells Angels. You don't have a job. The club is your career and they *expect* you to get arrested. Your friends, your family, they all live with the knowledge—maybe the dread—that you'll be behind bars eventually.

When you're a Hells Angel and you get arrested, you're not thinking about getting fired from your job or coming home to find your wife has put all your possessions on the front lawn. You're thinking about what the cops know, how you can get out of it and, above all else, keeping your mouth shut.

I was sitting at my dad's kitchen table while Sergeant Peter Casey of the York Regional Police and Sergeant Gregg Swiss of the Ontario Provincial Police read me the long list of charges. When they got to the part about conspiracy to traffic cocaine, I mentally ran through all of my activities and the possible scenarios that the police were aware of.

When Casey mentioned the dates involved, I noticed that they corresponded exactly to when I provided the pot and percs to Sheila. Since I had already figured out that she was the agent, it meant that what I had done with her was all they really had on me. They had no evidence that linked me to moving shit from Point A to Point B for Billy Dawson or TC (which was my primary job). And they knew nothing about me doing collections or fighting or anything else. I couldn't help it—I shouted, "BeBop's!" at almost exactly the same time my dad did. My dad could tell it was my involvement with BeBop's because of the names mentioned. Swiss knew what we were talking about, but didn't say anything because the house was still full of SWAT guys. But the look on his face spoke absolute volumes.

I felt relieved. Knowing that they only had evidence against me for those two piddly-ass transactions made my whole body relax. In fact, my mind even began to wander. I looked around at all the SWAT guys trying to look tough and chuckled to myself a bit because I knew for a fact that if my mom was still alive, each of them would have a cup of coffee in his hands, his shoes off—shoes were

not allowed inside her house—and a long list of chores to do before
he left. They were the same chores my dad probably would have
been doing before golf that day if the house had not been packed
tight as fuck with heavily armed and armored cops.

My dad told me to get a lawyer. That wasn't new—he had
gotten them before for both of us over the years. I'd seen a little bit
of minor trouble, going back to when I was a doorman, and he had
been stopped and charged for driving while impaired a couple of
times. Back then, hiring a lawyer for that kind of thing was money
well spent. There was still plenty of wiggle room in court before the
Breathalyzer became standard equipment. As a system, it worked
out for us.

I was marched out of the house—in front of everyone I had
grown up with—into a marked Toronto police car with the lights
flashing. So much for subtlety.

The cops hauled me up to the jail in Newmarket. It was already
rush hour by then, and it was clear that neither of them knew where
they were going. In fact, they got lost before they even made it as far
as the Toronto Zoo. I had to laugh, and told them I wouldn't tell
anyone about the mix-up if they didn't. Of course, I grew up in the
area, so I knew a shortcut to Newmarket and gave them directions. I
later joked that I should have sent them back to my place, but that's
where the shit they were looking for was.

They had searched the house, even brought a dog in to sniff
around. They didn't find anything, though. They even missed my
dad's old shotgun. He used to take it hunting and always joked that
the barrel must be bent because he never managed to hit anything.

175

When we finally got to the Newmarket jail, I saw a line of cop cars out front. They all had some pretty familiar-looking faces in their backseats.

I had never been in jail before. I had been arrested before, but I'd always been released on my own recognizance.

Almost as soon as I got there, they patted me down for weapons and searched me for contraband to confiscate. The strict definition of contraband varies from cop to cop, but it generally leaves you with nothing but your clothes—no wallet, no jewelry. And it can get pretty nitpicky. Forget shoelaces or any type of string in a hoodie or pants or anything. I was lucky, I guess, because when I walked into the holding cell wearing a zip-up hooded sweatshirt and a club shirt complete with logo, the other guys were amazed. "How the fuck did you get that through?" somebody asked, because they had all been stripped of their club gear after the cops said they could be used as evidence. I didn't know, so I just shrugged.

After the search and seizure, they walked me to the cell. I was surprised to see that it was a cement room with bars for a front wall and a swinging door. It looked just like the jails in the cowboy shows I watched on TV as a kid.

And inside was the whole fleet. That's the word that ran through my head when I saw them. All those guys who tried to look so tough in their gold jewelry and leather jackets on top of their Harleys now looked like a bunch of tired, old used cars that nobody wanted.

It was a real eye-opener for me. I looked at these guys whom I had always admired, had wanted to be like, and for the first time saw them the way almost everybody else did. I saw them for what they really were. All I could see was a bunch of lowlifes, really insecure drains on society. I looked at them, and all I could see were their hanging beer guts, their unkempt toenails and their overall disgusting appearance. And the smell. Immediately, my sense memory put me back to working the malls in downtown Toronto and how the worst of the worst smelled. I couldn't think of it any other way. I was locked in a room full of bums. And what made it worse was that they were my sworn brothers in arms. I was one of them.

The only one who looked like he might have belonged anywhere but a drunk tank or homeless shelter was BeBop Burton. When I walked into the cell, he was sitting with TC.

When I walked in, nobody greeted me the traditional biker way, with a hearty handshake and a hug. Nobody even stood up. Instead, they all just sat there, looking scared and barely acknowledging me.

That's when it dawned on me that TC's greed had gotten so out of hand that it had landed us all in jail. As I sat there, I saw more and more guys I knew being led into the cage. There was Bully, Doug Hoyle, Keith Gallagher, Bobby Prested, Adam Drake, Dave "The Duke" Blackwood and a long list of supporters. It seemed like it wasn't going to stop, as a constant stream of guys I knew rapidly filled the cell. We all started joking about it, because it really was a lot of guys—and smell—stuffed into a single room. At least we all still had our senses of humor.

The core guys the cops were after, of course, were club leaders like TC and Doug Hoyle, as well as the West End Montreal guys, who I figured were responsible for bringing the heat onto BeBop's in the first place.

Once the important guys were all there, we had a meeting to see if we could determine the identity of the informant. There was no way they could have gotten all of us without somebody working on the inside. At first, the guys had no idea, even though I had figured it out. But as the day went on, it became apparent to all of them that just one key player who had been involved in all the transactions was missing. It was Sheila, the waitress from BeBop's. And, sure enough, by the time they were transferring us to the West (as we called the Toronto West Detention Centre in Rexdale) for the weekend, she was nowhere to be found.

While we were being held, my girlfriend at the time was one of many people who kept trying to call Sheila, but her phone went straight to voice mail. I knew why. She was a police agent, making and recording deals to incriminate us all. Even though I was behind bars, I remember thinking, "Good for her. She got out of the life." I didn't feel any resentment or anger toward her. After all, she had tried to warn me.

To be honest, my big concern was what—out of all the shit I was doing at the time—the cops knew about and did not know about. I knew they were aware of the two insignificant sales connected to Sheila, but it dawned on me that they could add more charges at any time, especially if someone else panicked and talked. It was pretty traumatic to not know what they had on me.

I could have gotten in trouble for a union issue. Bully, who looked exactly like Don Cherry, had a buddy named Glenn. Glenn was a citizen who drove a truck for a living and knew a lot of people. One of his friends ran a construction-related company up in the

Woodbridge area. Apparently, the guy was under a lot of pressure from a union, and it looked like his employees were going to become part of some local. That would have cost him a ton, so Glenn went to Bully to see if he could help.

Bully, Glenn and I showed up at the company. The owner's office was at least as nice as any downtown Toronto CEO's I had ever seen. He clearly had cash to spare. As soon as the introductions were over, the guy got right to the point. His workers had been making noise about organizing, and he made it abundantly clear that he didn't want his shop to go union under any circumstances. Our job would be to intimidate the right people or pay them off—just make them go away.

I remember thinking, "What the fuck did Bully get me into?" I assured the guy I would speak to someone about his options, but I was a little pissed off at the same time. I tried to get him into a discussion about fair labor practices and pay for his workers, but he would not hear any of it. He was a rich man who wanted to get even richer, and there was no way he was going to let any union put a dent in that.

I had never done this kind of work before, but I did know a union guy named Ian Craig, who just happened to be TC's brother. I bought Ian a couple of beers and we discussed the situation. Ian said that there was a problem: No matter how the company's owner felt about it, his shop needed to be unionized. Most shops like his already were, and it was inevitable that his would be too. I couldn't help but agree with him.

Ian agreed to speak with the local union guy who was putting pressure on our guy. He was going to tell him that the owner was trying to hire two Hells Angels to scare the union off. But he was also going to tell him that Bully and I weren't stupid enough to stir up a whole union. So, basically, we weren't going to do anything to the union other than tip them off that the guy was trying to intimidate them.

But Bully—being an entrepreneur at heart—had to make some money off the deal. So we went back to the company and told the owner that for $10,000, we would talk to the union guy who was giving him trouble, but that we would make no guarantees. The money, we told him, was for our time and expenses entertaining some of the union guys and, if necessary, greasing some pockets. Even then, I took a few minutes to tell the guy that I believed that everyone connected to the shop, including him, would be much better off if he let the union in—it was the best way to ensure he had a safe and productive work environment. Again, he didn't want to hear it. And Bully wasn't too crazy about me potentially jinxing the deal because of my opinions.

It didn't matter what I said. The guy handed Bully and me $3,000 each on the spot. Glenn got nothing. Sorry, Glenn, you're a citizen and that's just how it goes.

Those are just the kinds of things Hells Angels do to make money. I didn't feel so bad. I made that asshole's wallet lighter, and the union came in anyway.

I was thinking about stuff like that when I was taken to West to wait for bail. Jail's not a lot of fun. Think about it this way: Even if you were at the poshest, most expensive hotel in the world, you'd hate it if you couldn't leave your room or make decisions about when you could eat or sleep. Now imagine that, but the posh hotel room is actually a filthy, soulless government building with shitty food.

I wasn't scared of jail. Why would I be? There are a few perks that go along with being a Hells Angel in the world of criminals. And that definitely includes jail. It's kind of different in the federal pen or provincial jail, but in waiting-for-trial jail, we had some stature. We didn't have to prove anything to anyone.

I knew that I wouldn't have to fight every single guy in there who considered himself to be a bad dude or a pugilist. But I knew I could take care of myself if I had to. I knew I was a pretty damn good knuckle-to-knuckle fighter, especially if there were no weapons involved. Fighting takes speed, skill and reach, and I still had all of those. Even if I was set upon by a bunch of guys, I knew I had enough in me to keep me in any fight and that I would never get completely wiped out. Hey, I've lost a few scraps in the past. Anyone who says he hasn't just isn't a fighter. You're not a winner if you haven't lost a least a little along the way. You know who wins fights? The guy who gives it his all and never gives up. Losers are the guys who try to get it over with quickly, the guys who take the cheap shots, the guys who kick and scratch and even pull weapons.

While I was thinking about that, the guys began to lighten up and start talking. As the number of guys coming in tailed off from a deluge to a trickle, we started to get a handle on what had happened. Eventually, we realized that it was a prospect from the Keswick chapter who had led them to BeBop's. And that's where they got to Sheila. And she began to help them. A lot.

After a while, I was allowed a phone call. I managed to get my dad. I told him I could be out as early as the following week and that I didn't want him to worry about getting me a lawyer. The club had its own lawyer. They retained a guy named Les Morris. He was a pretty good criminal lawyer, and we had supplied him with enough business that every member carried his name and number with them at all times.

My dad was clearly relieved, but also far from impressed. I knew that he would do anything and everything I needed. He and my girl-friend had become very close while my mom was dying, and they would come to visit me together—they'd make a nice family outing out of it. I was grateful for both of them at the time. I used to like to say that she was my rock and he was an oak.

Eventually, we all appeared before a judge. I was in the penalty box with Bully and some other guy. As the charges were read out, I thought to myself, *Holy shit—Bully and I are charged with almost identical offenses, even though our jobs with the club are very different.*

At first, it didn't make sense. But then I realized the cops' plan. They would cover us all in a blanket of conspiracy charges. Their hope was that when the guys saw that they were facing so many charges with the potential for long jail sentences, they would cave in and grab for a plea bargain or rat on the other guys.

Lots of guys do rat, and some other guys go the distance. After seeing everything I've seen, I can tell you that the latter group are the stupid ones. Trials, no matter what happens in the end, are always time-consuming and expensive. Going all the way with one will ruin you financially, and, if you do get convicted, a lot of bikers believe that the judge will usually tack on what we call the "stupid tax" to your sentence for wasting so much public money. I know that now; I didn't know it then.

Before the arrests went down, John Neal gave me some advice in case I was ever arrested. "Fight it all the way," he told me. "Don't say anything to a cop. Just wait them out. You're a biker, and they are just doing their job. You can beat just about anything if you let your lawyer and the Crown attorneys talk it over in their offices instead of in front of a judge."

I remembered his advice and planned on making it my strategy. A single pound of pot and a hundred percs? That was nothing. The conspiracy charges would almost certainly get tossed. It was clear that the cops wanted TC, Hoyle and the West End guys from Montreal. They were a lot less interested in Bully, me, Duke or Bobby Prested. We were in the pond, certainly, but not even considered to be medium-sized fish. They wanted the guys they thought were lunkers.

I was shocked when the judge said there would be no bail for me.

We were taken back to the cell and the next batch of accused went up to see the judge. Then we found out there would be no bail for anyone.

Later that day, they fed us. Much to my surprise, it wasn't a bad meal at all, considering it came from the world's favorite clown, Ronald McDonald.

As we all became a little less unnerved, I spoke with Duke about our duties as sergeants-at-arms. We decided it was our responsibility to keep not only our club brothers, but all of the associates safe from the guards and other inmates. And we agreed on one other thing: We were all behind bars because TC was a selfish prick who'd gotten us all busted by making Sheila's life so intolerable that she essentially had no choice but to turn informant.

We were chained at the wrists and ankles and taken back to the Toronto West Detention Centre. It was right in the middle of the SARS scare, and all government facilities had strict regulations about everything. Just to get into jail, everyone had to be screened (including having their temperature taken) and fill out a questionnaire regarding contact with other people and symptoms. That was the easy part. After the SARS screening came the traditional jailhouse strip-down, bend-over-and-cough screening, which everyone, of course, dreads.

Most of the staff at West were noncommunicative, almost like they were robots and your humanity just didn't register with them. But not all of them. I actually told one correctional officer that it was my first time in jail. He laughed and told me he'd explain how things worked. I felt relieved. The last thing I wanted was to make enemies out of the same people who were housing and feeding us. I asked when I would have to bend over and spread 'em. I wasn't looking forward to it, because I had been dragged out of bed before 6 a.m. and hadn't showered in a while. Besides, I pointed out, the toilet paper at the Newmarket jail was not exactly an ideal way to keep the ol' back door clean.

He laughed and told me that they didn't check the Hells Angels that closely. He knew that we never bothered to hoop anything into jail because we had so many people—old ladies, wannabes, maybe even some lawyers—who would do it for us.

That was cool by me. This guy, I thought, would not be looking up my smelly old ass. Just another benefit of membership.

As we were sitting there in chains, waiting for our names to be called, Jeff "Buds" McIlmurray stood up and started yelling at the guards. He would point at them individually and shout, "Fuck you, you, you and definitely fuck you, you asshole."

I thought it was an idiotic move because, right away, like dogs waiting to pounce, the guards were upon him and hauling him away to a private cell. But then I realized his plan. McIlmurray was a Keswick member and a seasoned con. He knew that a nice, quiet solitary cell was the best way for him to spend his weekend. He knew what he had done to end up in jail and he also knew there would be no wriggling out of it. Once he saw there would be no bail for him, he decided to start on a plea bargain ASAP and begin doing his time right away. He never admitted to the police that he was a Hells Angel. It was a smart move that allowed him to accept a plea bargain to the best deal his lawyer could get right away, and it also prevented the feds from looking into his bank accounts and shit like that. McIlmurray did a little time, sure, but he saved a shitload of money and was free to get back to business as soon as he was out again.

At 10 p.m., my name was called along with a few others. We were escorted, single file (like toddlers on a school field trip), through the range to our cells. I was unhappy, but not surprised, to see that my cell had two bunks and two guys already in them. That meant I was on the floor. Hells Angels do get certain benefits, but the rules are different in jail. I had no right to ask some guy to give up his bunk for me, and I would never ask him to. I was a guest in their house.

I introduced myself. They were a couple of small-time serial boosters—what we call shoplifters—who were doing a bit for one conviction while waiting for trial on another set of charges. They immediately asked if I was part of the biker bust. I told them that

I was, and reintroduced myself in the traditional Hells Angels style: "Hi, I'm Shaky from Downtown Toronto." They were not impressed. There are large parts of the criminal world who don't want to deal with bikers because they have a reputation for bringing the heat. But one of the guys knew a Hells Angel who had come up with the Olive Street Crips, so at least we had something in common. They admitted that their friend in the club would want them to take care of one of his brothers, as long as that brother wasn't being a dick and just did his time.

Floor or not, I slept like a baby on my first night in jail. But my cellmates weren't so lucky. Due to the family curse, I snore like a freight train.

The boosters were probably delighted the next morning when I was moved to another cell. To my surprise, I was taken to a different range, and all the guys I knew were there. Funny thing was, we were having a boys' weekend after all, even though we weren't exactly fishing and drinking up at the cottage.

11

A NEW PLAN

Jail was pretty tolerable for a couple of reasons. The first was that I was in West, which was kind of a decent place, at least compared to the old Don Jail, where some of the guys—like Ian Watson and Doug Hoyle—were taken. And, second, the guys inside mostly kept to themselves.

My cellmate was Dave "The Duke" Blackwood. I never did find out why they put all of us who were fortunate enough to be in West in the same range.

Friday went okay. To our surprise, there were just the two of us in a cell designed for two (I had heard that was rare). We spent the day talking. Dave told me about Newfoundland, his hometown and fishing. He spoke at length about how much he loved his girl, Wendy. I remember that I spoke a lot about my dad and how sorry I was for all the shit I'd put him through.

All in all, it wasn't that bad. Eventually, we got around to the elephant in the room: TC. I was pissed. I went off about how selfish, violent and out of control TC had been, all in the pursuit of more and more money. I told Dave that I was absolutely sure that if he had been able to control his greed and operate under the radar with just a modicum of self-control, none of us would be in this mess, with criminal records hanging over our heads. I still believe that even now.

Dave had a much better handle on the politics of the biker world, and he assured me that once we were all free on bail, parole or whatever, there would be a sit-down and TC would have to answer to everyone in the chapter.

He also told me that everything I did was being watched. Jail time was a test, just like prospecting was. And it wasn't just the eyes of our club that were on me, but other clubs and crews, guards in jail and cops involved with the case. They would watch me constantly to see how I conducted myself inside. A lot of guys—lawbreakers and those in law enforcement alike—would love to see a Hells Angel lose his shit behind bars.

Bully spoke to us about what was going to happen next. We were instructed not to worry about the charges and to let the lawyers do the work they were paid to do. Instead, our job would be to do our time uneventfully and to prepare our case against TC for President Winner to hear.

It wouldn't be hard. I mean, holy shit, the guy was moving fifteen keys a week with a Toronto connection and even more from Montreal. And he'd pissed off a whole lot of people by pinching pennies and arguing about twenty measly bucks here and there.

You learn a lot about how jail works and the hierarchies inside on your first days after the doors shut. The most important guy on a range is known as the quarterman. He is usually the guy who has been inside the longest (either awaiting trial or on short-term detention), and he controls the activity on the range, keeping people in line no matter what club they are with. He is also responsible for serving food and determining who gets what and when.

Our quarterman on our range at West was a guy named Reggie. Luckily, the Tommies—Tommy "Chubs" Bogiatzis and Tommy "Fatty" Christodoulo—had already vouched for me. Both Tommies were Scarborough guys who also happened to be big-time coke dealers. They were among the first guys in the Toronto area to deal with Stadnick and the Hells Angels in the 1990s. At the time, the Vagabonds MC and, to a lesser extent, the Para-Dice Riders told everyone not to deal with the Hells Angels. The Vagabonds were still upset over how the Hells Angels had assassinated their president, Snorkel Melanson, over his drug debts in the 1980s. But that wasn't common knowledge. Back then, it didn't seem like people cared much when a drug dealer was murdered. There was no big investigation, no arrests, no nothing. The Tommies didn't care what the local gangs wanted when the lure of cocaine from Montreal came into town.

So before too long, Reggie came up to me and told me how things worked. The older guys always ate first and we made sure that anyone who had any dietary issues got whatever they needed.

We made sure our guys got enough to eat while Reggie kept ours for us. Bully went ballistic when he found out that TC had offered extra peanut butter to some guy he didn't know. Bully was in his sixties and low on energy and really could have used that peanut butter, and

TC wanted to give it to some crook booster who just happened to be arrested on the same night as us? Fuck him, said Bully.

It wasn't hard to figure out what was really going on. TC knew that we would almost certainly get bail, and that he would not, so he was paving the way for his long stay in jail to be more comfortable. He needed new friends, and lots of them, quickly because it was pretty clear he was running out of old friends. He might have been a prick and a coward, but he certainly knew how to survive.

We also had to distribute meds. On your way into jail, the guards ask you what meds you're on and for what illness. At the size I was, my blood pressure was through the roof, so I got the pills I needed— easy, cheap and non-narcotic. Bully had the same problem, and got the same pills. TC, though, was still recovering from his liver transplant, so he needed all kinds of shit.

I spent Saturday and Sunday pacing the range with Bully, talking about the bait we were going to use the next time we went fishing. There was a TV on the range, and Bully found a fishing show, so we all gathered around, giving the guys on the show advice and saying things like "That's what I woulda done" when we agreed with their methods.

It wasn't all that bad inside West, unlike what our boys were experiencing at the Don. I heard that Hoyle was walking around on their range and asked the biggest guy he could find who the quarterman was. By coincidence, the guy he was asking *was* the quarterman, so Hoyle dropped him with one punch. That's just how they did things in the Don.

On Sunday night, just before we had to all go back to our own cells and turn in for the night, I was out on the range when some guy with a mop and pail slipped a rolled-up wad of paper towel under the door and whispered, "It's for Reggie." I said okay and kept the paper towel safe until I saw Reggie. When I found him, I covertly handed him the package.

Inside were pain meds—the real strong ones that make percs feel like children's Aspirin. He gave me some to dish out. Bully got one, so did Dave the Duke and Dave the Dog, and of course I saved one for myself. We all enjoyed a much better night's sleep than you'd expect guys in jail to.

I knew better than to go anywhere near TC that weekend. Like pretty well everyone else, I was just too angry, and I didn't want to do anything I might regret later. Dave the Dog told me he would have taken him down already if he weren't a transplant patient. Dave was not a member, but we all knew him. He was a tough rounder who, I was told, moved a lot of pot and stolen items. He was said to be a career criminal, and he had learned a little more with every conviction. He was livid because he knew that it was TC's carelessness that had put us all behind bars. He said that if it weren't for TC, we would have all sailed happily beneath the cops' radar for as long as we wanted.

On Monday morning, we were all rounded up and taken to the Newmarket courthouse for our bail hearings. It was a gorgeous day, but we only saw it from a sally port and through the windows of the caged van we were riding in. Bully and I were handcuffed, and he asked one of the guards if he could ride up front with her. She laughed and said sure. Bully then told her that I would drive if she wanted me to. He could always be funny, and he knew exactly how to lighten the mood.

I don't know how she knew, but the guard told us that it looked like a good day for us and said we would probably get bail. That prospect brightened our spirits. Going to court and potentially home sure beat sitting and stewing in West like TC and Dave the Dog were. There was no way TC would get bail with all they had against him, and the Dog had a history of trafficking convictions, so that meant an automatic rejection of his first attempt at bail. Bully and I, on the other hand, were golden. Over his sixty years, Bully had spent almost a year behind bars here and there, and I had never seen the inside of a jail until that weekend.

When we arrived in Newmarket, I met with my lawyer. BeBop and Bully were there too. The lawyer told us that it was a huge case—they had arrested eighty people—so the Crown wouldn't be able to even begin to get his shit together for two years at least. That delighted Bully. He said he had it all figured out and that we would be fine, and that the charges would probably be stayed after a year or so if we agreed to the Crown's stipulations. Later, he plea-bargained down, took a slap on the wrist and was back with the club in less than a year.

We were led into court in front of a judge. From the box, I could see my dad sitting with the wives of some of the other members, a few friends, and a guy I recognized as a cop.

My bail was huge. I was released and my stipulations were pretty standard, from what I have been told. I had to obey a curfew, I couldn't drink in public, couldn't have a cell phone or a pager, and couldn't associate with known criminals or club members. And I had to reside at my dad's house. I was actually allowed out after curfew, but only if my dad was with me.

During the hearing, my dad asked the Crown if it was okay if he took me to the Keg, because every man needs a good meal and neither of us knows how to cook. Years later, I was dealing with the same Crown and he brought that up. We both laughed.

After I was released, we waited outside to see who else got out. While I was there, I saw Toronto detective Al Rennie having a smoke. I went up to him and told him that I knew that it was Sheila who was the agent who turned us all in, and that I harbored no ill will against her for what she had done. It was the best thing for her in the circumstances she was in, and she certainly wasn't to blame for any of the stuff we were doing. He didn't say anything. He couldn't—he was too shocked—as he shook his head.

From there, my dad and I went directly to the Keg. He put away a mug of draft pretty quickly and followed it with a vodka and water. I told him that was a good way to start his day. He told me to shut up and that we could both use a little stress relief.

I did drink my beer, and I ate a lot of beef and potatoes. Even a few days of jail food is too much.

After the Keg, we went to a pub called Purdy's. Some of the friends my dad had made after he met his new girlfriend were there. I was kind of self-conscious that I was still in the clothes I had been arrested in, so when I eventually made it back to Dad's, I showered and put on some fresh clothes before cracking a beer and sitting out in the backyard.

I was contemplating my situation when my girlfriend dropped by. My dad was off with his girl, so we could talk. She told me that she hadn't signed up for this. She hadn't, it's true, but she certainly didn't mind it when things were working. I decided that, whatever happened, there were two things I'd never do: snitch or quit the club while I was on charges. I was determined to ride it out.

The next day, I searched my dad's house for cash, but it was all gone. The cops might miss a lot, but they never seem to leave any cash behind. I had some accounts receivable on the streets, so I went on a collections run.

I needed a quick $5,000 for bail fees, so I got that right away. Then I got a call from Les Morris, the club's lawyer. He wanted to see me at his office right away. When I got there, I was escorted upstairs into an office. At a boardroom table were Les, John "Winner" Neal, Doug Myles and a guy I didn't recognize. He was Ed Gresik, and he was soon to be my lawyer.

The first thing they told me was to take my stips (the stipulations of our agreement) seriously and to follow them to the letter or I would be back in jail. Then Les showed me the forty boxes of evidence the Crown had on me.

I couldn't look at any of it just yet. Winner, the president, had dibs. Ostensibly, it was John's job to look out for all of the chapter's members, but even then I knew that John was just protecting himself. He was making sure that none of the accused had mentioned him in the hours and hours of audio intercepts.

Because of my stips, there was no way I could make money the way I had become accustomed to. I needed to work, not just for the money, but for my peace of mind. Of all the people I knew, it was WR, my old security boss, who stepped up. He said that what I had learned by being a Hells Angel had value in the security industry, as well as to the police. I could leverage my way not just out of the club, but into some big money. I told him that wasn't going to happen.

But my time with his company had made me some good connections and had taught me to be a pretty good salesman. So when Sean Dodds offered me a job at the Yonge Street location of his Spy Depot store, I jumped at it. Spy Depot sells security devices and "novelties" like a hidden-video camera that can fit behind a necktie and record through a hole almost invisible to the naked eye. All legal.

It was my job to open the store up at nine in the morning and close it at five thirty. In between, I would sell small, easy-to-assemble alarm systems, hidden safes and, of course, investigation services. It was a good gig. No weekends, $500 a week and any side cash I could make—although not really Spy Depot's main business, customers with security-related needs came in from time to time, and I was able to negotiate this work directly with them.

While I was there, a very pretty young woman who was clearly upset told us that she was suspicious that somebody was entering her apartment during the day, while she was at work, and rummaging around but not stealing anything. Sean and I immediately knew what was going on. It was clearly someone who had a key to the apartment, because there were no signs of forced entry. And because nothing was stolen, we were certain that the motive was some kind of sexual-deviant shit.

She didn't believe it, or didn't want to. But we convinced her to take a "nanny cam," a hidden-video recording device that parents often use to check out what babysitters do when they're not around.

This one was hidden inside a pretty ordinary-looking clock, and we told her to put it in her bedroom.

Two weeks later, we saw her again. She had brought the disk from the nanny cam. And, sure enough, the superintendent from her building had been entering her unit, going through her dirty laundry hamper and jerking off. She was extremely grateful, and gave us a big cash tip for solving the great mystery.

Sean was a good guy, and we split the tip 50/50. He was a graduate of St. Mike's College in Toronto and then went to Niagara College to play basketball. He was, after all, six foot ten. As I recall, a couple of his kids played college football.

He was also very knowledgeable when it came to the business. One time while I was there, a Jamaican guy came in, all excited. He had been convinced that his business partner was not only fucking his wife, but was also a police informant. He wanted his car swept for bugs as soon as possible. His partner had borrowed the car the previous day, and that made our client very suspicious.

Between the two of us, we knew exactly which few places the cops would place a transmitter, and sure enough, there was one. The guy gave us $1,000—not bad for less than five minutes' work.

Sean had a partner he owned Spy Depot with, a guy who knew Peter Scarcella really well. If you don't know who Pietro "Peter" Scarcella is, I can tell you that many people believed he was the Mafia's top guy in Toronto. He came to Canada from Sicily when he was a kid in the 1970s and started his Mafia career as a driver for Toronto don Paul Volpe. Volpe had a big mouth and a lot of debts back east, and his body was found in the trunk of his wife's BMW, parked in a lot at Pearson

International Airport in 1983. After that, Scarcella rose through the ranks in Toronto, becoming famous for talking his way out of a sanctioned hit, and I had heard that he had close ties to members of the Rizzuto and Commisso crime organizations.

At the time, Peter told his friend that he felt as though he had a threat against him, so he was looking for a little personal security. Sean suggested that I handle it. After all, I was experienced in personal protection, and I was good at keeping my mouth shut. I was up for it, so I met with Peter at a nice restaurant where we could discuss the threat.

Peter was actually a very unassuming guy, very quiet. Instead, this guy named Sam did all the talking. He was a stereotype, looking and acting just like the mob guys you see in movies and on TV. It was obvious he was coming up and wanted to make a positive impression on his boss.

They told me that Peter needed a bodyguard because of a recent business deal that had not gone as planned. He was fine during the day, Sam told me, but he was worried about nights, when he was at home with his wife.

It sounded like an easy enough job, so I agreed on the condition that he rent me a nice car.

There was one hurdle, though. One of my court-ordered stipulations was that I could not be out after dark unless my dad was with me. I couldn't very well take him on the job, so I asked my lawyer to ask the court for a variance on my bail conditions to allow me to work at night. It was granted, with the result that a Hells Angel charged with trafficking was allowed to be out at night as long as he was protecting a mafioso.

After that was cleared up, I went to Peter's house. He met me in the driveway. He was clear that he wanted a bodyguard, but he refused to tell me any specifics about the potential threats he faced. The No. 1 rule for professionals who protect people is that they have to know exactly what threats exist so that they can plan accordingly. The whole plan—including the need for manpower and equipment—hinges on that knowledge. But Peter refused to budge. That, of course, made me think he was lying to me somewhere along the line. I didn't like him. He struck me as both cheap and insincere. But for $50 an hour and a chance to work again, I had no choice but to take it. All I could do was use my instincts and hope for the best.

I told him I'd show up every night, just to let him know I was there. Then I would move around, because staying in one spot would get me burned by any bad guys and they could just plan around me by staying out of my sight and hearing. I'd be gone by the light of day, not just because I could get spotted by the threat, but I wanted to make sure I did not come close to breaking any of my bail conditions.

To get ready for the job, I did the usual self-preparation course on urban geography. I plotted the quickest routes to the nearest hospital and police station. I familiarized myself with all his neighbors' cars so that any vehicle from outside would become instantly recognizable.

Of course, Peter had a palatial estate. I got to know his house inside and out and planned escape routes for him and entry points for me. I knew every window and door like I'd lived there for years.

I also interviewed him on his own personal security plan. He told me that he and his wife were usually home at night and that he had a few guns. His plan was that if anyone entered, he'd blow them away. That's when he warned me to stay away from his doors and windows at night. *No shit, Sherlock*, I thought to myself.

The first night was taken up mostly by gathering intel. I put everything I knew into an old Perly's map of the area. If I had lost it, it wouldn't mean anything to whoever picked it up, but it was a treasure trove of data for me.

My plan was to position myself in various locations from which I could keep an eye on the house while remaining inconspicuous. For the most part, my job was simply to sit tight and keep my eyes open. It was, essentially, a whole lot of doing nothing.

Some people can do that, some can't. After a few nights with nothing happening, I brought Sean Buchanan along. Not only would he keep me company, I thought, but I could teach him the trade. Sean was a full patch from West Toronto. He had been with Downtown, but left because of a family relationship—he married Winner's daughter.

On Sean's first night, we had been discussing club business for a while when I saw Peter get into his car and start driving around. It quickly became obvious he was looking for us. He could have called me if he needed anything, but his leisurely driving indicated that he was cruising around the neighborhood, trying to determine if we were ripping him off or not. He wanted to see if I was one of those guys who would just take his money and not show up.

He didn't find us, and you can bet he was plenty pissed. So when I went to meet him in his driveway the following dawn, I didn't let him talk. I told him I saw him driving around looking for us and showed him pictures of himself in his car to prove it. His mood quickly changed. I could tell he was begrudgingly impressed. If I could watch him look for us completely undetected, I stood a very good chance of keeping him safe from any bad guys.

Sean did not like surveillance work. He described it as "sitting around and doing fuck all." I didn't blame him. Like I said, some people can do it, some can't. I also tried a couple of other guys, but they weren't into it, either.

I didn't know it at the time, but Peter was caught up in a huge mess. A Sicilian pal of his who was in Canada on a fake passport, Michele Modica, owed $240,000 to computer genius Mark Peretz. Peretz was not in the Mafia or the Hells Angels, but he had made a lot of money for both of them through offshore online gambling and had a foolproof business laundering cash through ATMs. He commanded a lot of respect on the streets, and while he was no tough guy himself, he had a phalanx of ass-kickers for anyone who crossed him.

Later, Toronto police would tell reporters that the friendship between Scarcella and Modica was like "Velcro," but Peter began to get pissed off with his old buddy when he refused to pay Peretz and when he brought in another pal from New York to operate on Peter's turf without telling him. The bugger had even used the money he owed Peretz to get his American friend established.

At a meeting of Toronto gangsters, Peter told the crowd he was "wiping his hands" when it came to Modica, which meant he no longer offered him any kind of relationship, effectively rescinding any protection from Peretz.

It was actually more than that.

I later found out that Peretz's bodyguard, Paris Christoforou, had kicked Modica in the face and put a gun in his mouth when he tracked him down. Christoforou just happened to also be sergeant-at-arms of the North Toronto chapter of the Hells Angels. Because of that association, the *Globe and Mail* later called Peretz a "biker," but I don't think he'd ever been on a motorcycle in his life. Christoforou told Modica that if he didn't come up with at least $130,000 in two days, he was a dead man.

It was all going down while I was working for Peter. He was pretty sure Peretz would send someone after him because it was well known that he had a close relationship with Modica. Or that Modica would try to off him pre-emptively.

Instead, two Mafia guys, along with Christoforou and a friend of his, Antonio "Jelly" Borrelli, met at a shitty doughnut shop in North York to discuss a plan. The Mafia guys would lead Christoforou and Borrelli to Modica and they would do what they were paid to do.

It was a huge disaster. The Mafia guys located Modica at a place called California Sandwiches and tipped off their associates. There was some confusion as to who was who, and Christoforou and Borelli were pretty sure Modica had just left, so they started shooting up the place out of anger and frustration. They had five guns—including a Colt semiautomatic rifle—all acquired from Peter.

Louise Russo, an innocent bystander who had been standing in line, had one bullet graze her head and another one enter her spine between her shoulder blades.

After Christoforou and Borrelli fled, one of the Mafia guys—Raffaele Delle Donne—came out from the closet he'd jumped into as a hiding place when the bullets started flying. He saw Russo helpless on the ground, desperately trying to grab her cell phone and screaming, "Where's my daughter?" Delle Donne picked up her phone and called 911. Not only was he shocked that Russo had been shot for no reason, but he was pissed off that he had very nearly been hit.

It could not possibly have gone worse. Talk about a sympathetic victim. Russo was a mom who had taken a day off from her job at Bell Canada to take care of one daughter who had cerebral palsy and to celebrate the fact her other daughter had just earned her stripes as an air cadet. She had stopped in California Sandwiches to grab her younger daughter—the cadet, who was waiting in Russo's car in the parking lot and had missed dinner—a nice, warm veal parm. If the Hells Angels wanted to stay out of the news after the mass arrests, getting involved with a mob hit, fucking it up and paralyzing an innocent woman was no way to go about it.

But I didn't know any of that at the time. It would have been nice to know how deep the shit was while I was driving around, watching out for this guy while I was totally unarmed. All I knew at the time was that Peter was scared someone was out to get him. And someone was: the police.

Delle Donne, disgusted by what he had been a part of, turned police agent and gathered evidence about the conspirators. Peter got eleven years for putting the whole thing in motion; Borrelli, the triggerman, got twelve; Peretz and Christoforou, who fired one shot but didn't hit anything, also got eleven each. They were all out by the end of 2012. As part of a plea deal that was signed off on by Attorney General Michael Bryant, many people in the Toronto region who were family, friends or business associates of the convicted men held a fundraising drive for Russo and handed her $2 million in cash.

I'd say it was karma for Peter and his friends, but the funny part is that Modica went back to Italy, unharmed and not a penny lighter in his wallet. He was later arrested in Sicily after two Spanish mafiosi were assassinated there, but managed to wriggle out of the charges.

So I was back to working days at the store. After I would close the Spy Depot on weekdays, I would grab a green tea for the trip home and be back at my dad's by 6:16. Once I got there, I would crack a beer and then Conan, Glenn or the girl I was seeing at the time would come over. We'd grill some meat, have a few more beers and turn in early.

Every few months while I was out on stips, I'd have to go to court. There was usually no reason for me to be there; my name wouldn't even be mentioned. But all of the people arrested at the time—the cops called it Project Shirlea—went through the same thing. Little by little, our numbers would fall because the Crown would drop the charges against the small fry. They only have so much in the way of time and resources, and they don't bother with the petty stuff. If they can't get those guys to talk, they just let them go.

Except when it came to me. My charges were small, but there was no way they were letting me go. I was a full-patch Hells Angel and it was the duty of the cops and the Crown to disrupt the club as much as possible.

There was one good part to the court visits, though. It was the only time everyone in the club saw one another, and we could communicate pretty openly as long as there was a lawyer present.

On those dates, the Newmarket courthouse was jammed with those accused in Project Shirlea, their wives, girlfriends, friends and family. Usually, we all had a pretty good time. Say what you will about bikers, they know how to laugh in the face of adversity.

One of the items that was seized in the raid was my dad's computer. I knew a number of Durham cops from my time as a doorman in Pickering and some others from my high school. One of them, a guy named Don Patrick, saw me and asked me how my dad was doing. I told him he was okay, but that I was pretty pissed that the cops were holding on to my dad's computer. I mean, he wasn't charged with anything, so why shouldn't he have his stuff? Don agreed, and the next time my dad and I saw him, he promised to get my dad's computer back for him.

Just as we were talking, Lorne Campbell abruptly stuck his nose into the conversation. He pointed at Don and said, "This man is not your friend; he wants to put you in jail for as long as he can." He then proceeded to give me a humiliating dressing-down right there in front of my father. I would later learn that Campbell had never had much of a relationship with his own father, so he was not aware of how normal father-son dynamics worked.

I was so angry that my eyes were welling up. I was so full of energy from rage that it was a good thing for Lorne that we were in court, where there was fuck all I could do. I calmed down enough to explain what was going on, and Lorne softened his stance. He shook my dad's hand, but did not apologize.

Don kept his word, though. And my dad got his computer back later that same week—monitor, keyboard, cords and all.

My day in court came after twenty months of living with stips. I was shocked and delighted that the charges were stayed. I was sure they had enough evidence to convict me, but for reasons I was never told, I was free. After signing some papers, I walked out without any charges, any stipulations or any record. Years later, a cop told me that I was considered a small fish when it came to trafficking.

Later that night, I went to the clubhouse for the first time in almost two years. I didn't have a key, so I knocked on the door.

It was opened by a stout, bald man who was shaped like a fireplug. He stood his ground. Normally, if someone stood in my way, I'd just put them down. But I knew it was a bad idea here. First of all, I knew this guy was doing a security shift for the club and had no idea who I was. And second, I needed all the friends I could get, and that was no way to start making them. So I introduced myself as Shaky Dave. After a few questions to confirm my identity, he let me in and told me his name was Kenny. I would later learn that he was a skilled rider, a great backyard mechanic and had a citizen job as a service tech.

I had a beer with Kenny, who was a hangaround at that point, and swapped some stories. I knew right from the start that he was an okay guy and would definitely be a strong member of the club. He had an ability to listen, and that's important in the Hells Angels. You'd never find him trying to dominate a conversation or pretending to care what you were saying. He was a genuine guy who always kept his word. We ended up calling him Oil Can Kenny.

He wasn't the only one there. In many ways, Robin Moulton was the polar opposite of Oil Can Kenny. He was ambitious, phony and gave the minimum amount of respect, just enough to keep from getting kicked out of the club. Mark Staples had brought him around, and I could see right through him almost immediately.

Kenny and I downed a few beers before he told me he had to leave. His security shift was coming to an end and he had to get up early for his civilian job the next day. As he left, he asked me if I needed anything. That really impressed me, and I knew that he was the kind of guy who could show respect without kissing ass.

Oil Can Kenny's replacement turned out to be Patrick "Red" Fox, who came by with another guy named Gus Lawrence. They were both old school friends of John Neal's boys, who were full-patch members by then. They had some blow on them, so the good times were starting to roll and I really felt welcomed back.

Later, Billy Talbot called to congratulate me on being free. He was an old Satan's Choice guy and by then had become president of the Keswick chapter. He and another member, named Gary, went out of their way to set me up again. They got me some hash and even a new set of colors because the cops had seized mine.

It was then that Talbot told me what kind of shit TC had gotten himself into. The consensus—even among other chapters—was that he had gotten too greedy, and that was why we'd all been caught. He also told me I was going to have to work hard to shake the stink that years of association with TC had given me if I ever expected anyone to want to deal with me again.

The following night, there was a fundraising party for another member (there wasn't one for me), and I chatted with several other members about where I stood. It was all the same. They had no specific beef with me, but were wary of me because TC had been my sponsor, we had been great pals and we had done a lot of business together. It's not like I could have stopped him, but I understood.

Able to spend a night away from my dad's for the first time in a long while, I decided to drop in on the girl I was seeing then. I was walking down the Danforth when a van slid up next to me, the door flung open and the passenger shouted out, "Atwell!"

My first thought was, *Shit, am I being busted again?* Then the idea that it was a hit flashed through my mind.

It was neither. The guy shouting my name was Mike Press, a special constable with the Toronto police's guns-and-gangs unit. I had actually known Mike for years. Long before he was a cop, he was my boss at the Pickering Town Centre. We had a lot of fun back in those days. We had the same mindset: keep the mall safe and douchebag-free by any means necessary. He was a tall, muscular guy, a nondrinker and a faithful husband and father.

Once he got out of the van, Mike and I embraced. I could see that the cop who was driving the van had a very concerned look on his face. But Mike introduced me to him, Woody, and I eagerly shook his hand. We had a brief and casual conversation about family, health and stuff like that—just catching up, really—and then I left.

That night, I'd gone to my first church meeting since I was arrested. Everyone welcomed me back, with what I could tell were varying levels of sincerity. Afterward, I partied with Daryl Smith, Oil Can Kenny and Mehrdad "Juicy" Bahman.

At the meeting, I was reinstated as sergeant-at-arms, and my new job was to oversee the Red Line Crew, a support club we had started in Scarborough. Support clubs often do the work Hells Angels don't want to, and the guys in the support club do it because they think it'll get them into the big club. It works a lot like the minor leagues in baseball or hockey. It gives the big club a chance to watch these guys in action and see if they are trustworthy. Some guys fail in support clubs, some graduate to the big club and some guys make a career out of it. Doug Hoyle, Dave the Duke and I were tasked with the role of guiding the guys in the Red Line Crew into the life of the 1-percenter.

I was fine with that, but it was followed by a very unpleasant surprise. Winner handed me a bill. Of course, when a member is in jail, he doesn't have to pay his dues, but when he's on the street he does, and mine had been piling up while I was out on stips.

Doug said that Winner was being ridiculous.

Winner didn't try to explain the charge, but instead went into a speech about how important it is to pay club lawyers because we never know when members will need them, and we want them to step up at a moment's notice without any hesitation.

Frustrated, I went to the lawyer's office the next day. The only thing he said to me was to get the forty boxes of disclosure evidence the fuck out of his office because they were taking up too much room. "Where the fuck am I going to put forty more boxes of evidence?" I asked him. My dad's garage was full, man.

12

BACK IN THE LIFE

I was free, but I wasn't really. After the arrest, I began to see the club in an entirely different perspective. The guys weren't Hells Angels because they wanted to ride bikes and have a good time together; they were all in it for themselves. TC's insatiable greed had gotten us all in big trouble, and when it did, every guy just seemed to want to take the easiest way out, no matter who got hurt. And as soon as the charges against me were stayed, I was expected to go back to work for the club—after all, they had essentially ruined my ability to work for anyone else—and pay a huge bill even before I got back to my job. I was trapped, not by bars, but by the limitations the club had put on me and my life.

Just a few years ago, I was happy in my security career and loved making a few bucks on the side with the clubs. Riding and partying with the Para-Dice Riders, the Vagabonds and Satan's Choice made it even better. But, after the patch-over, after I became a Hells Angel, that all changed. I had no career—unless you count being a criminal—I had been behind bars, I had disrupted the lives of everyone I cared about and I had to break up with a woman I really cared about because my being in the club had endangered her career. I had become a bum surrounded by bums. It wasn't fun. I wasn't rich. I had had enough.

I wanted out. I knew it wouldn't be easy. I couldn't just quit. Then I would just be an ex–Hells Angel whose name had been in every newspaper. In the media, I was convicted. It didn't matter that the charges were stayed. That might make looking for a job tough. I had no skills other than security, and nobody would hire me for that because of my affiliation with the club.

I had no choice but to stick it out with the club and wait for something miraculous to happen.

When winter rolled around, it was time for club elections, and I was voted in as sergeant-at-arms again. That meant that I attended all the officers' meetings as well as the ordinary church meetings, and I got to know Donny Petersen, who was elected as national spokesman again, much better.

As most people who know anything about bikers in Canada are already aware, Donny is an eloquent speaker who can skillfully articulate his positions in just about any debate, even if he can fall into blatant narcissism from time to time.

He had been a biker since his late teens, when he joined the Para-Dice Riders. I was too young to know anything about him then, but I did know that his nickname was Sleaze. Nicknames are given to you very early in your biker career and tend to stick, even if they aren't actually reflective of your personality anymore. So I guess

Donny reinvented himself over the years, because I had never seen him do anything that could be described as even remotely sleazy. I'd call him classy, studied or quiet, but definitely not sleazy. Maybe it was an ironic nickname.

More than anyone else in the club, he was a true motorcycle enthusiast. He knew more about Harley-Davidsons, it seemed, than the people who made them. He wrote a number of books about motorcycle maintenance, and has flown all over the world teaching others his craft.

I knew that he started every day with a walk, just to clear his head before he began the day. It seemed to me that Donny had the gift of being able to start every day fresh. He had the ability to keep any shit from the past from sticking to him and he was always able to simply let the chips fall where they may. Along with that, he was incredibly regimented, whether it came to working out, furthering his career or communicating his knowledge or beliefs.

At the time, we were in what we called a period of a high level of awareness. That meant we had to keep security tight to prevent any information about ourselves or the club from leaking out. I had a guest speaker I knew give a lecture on sophisticated countersur-veillance techniques. I watched as Donny took notes and listened as intently as though the speaker was talking about valves on Harley-Davidson's new 109-cubic-inch engine.

After the lecture, while Donny had a Molson Canadian draft and I had a Guinness. I asked him what he thought of the speaker. He was fine, Donny told me, very informative. He also told me he agreed with the speaker's assertion that any good security program should cause a little inconvenience to the user because it reminds them to do their part regularly. That, he said, was particularly important to us because bikers, by nature, are lazy. And that, he told me, is why they get caught.

But Donny never worried about getting caught for one simple reason: he never broke the law. He told me that he had nothing to hide because he wasn't doing anything illegal, so he was not as concerned about his own security enough to alter his schedule to accommodate any special measures. "Let the cops follow me," he said. "It would be a huge waste of their time and money."

I believed him.

I was also in touch with WR. He had attended every court appearance I had made. He made it clear that he was there to support me, not the club. Not only did he want to know what was happening to me, but he found the whole process to be fascinating. Later, after I was freed, we'd meet for a beer and he'd always tell me to get out of the club, to just walk away and start over. I told him that I wanted to, but that I couldn't yet because I really needed something else to fall back on, and jobs for a guy like me were scarce at best.

One day, I was walking to Spy Depot when a well-dressed guy came up to me and handed me his business card. It had a federal investigator's logo on it, and he told me that if I ever wanted to talk, I should call him.

When I arrived at work, I showed Sean Dodds the card. He was skeptical, finding the situation and the card itself quite suspicious. More than a few things seemed amiss. We both knew that's not how cops worked. He told me it was probably a setup, or maybe a test from the club or someone in it. It seemed to him as though some-body in the club wanted to know if I'd talk or not.

So I showed the card to Doug Myles and Donny. Doug played it off like it was no big deal and said that it was commonplace for a guy facing time to squeal to save his own ass. I pointed out that I hardly fit that description, considering that the charges against me, which were weak to start with, had already been stayed. Not only was I not look-ing at any time, but I didn't even have a record. They shrugged it off.

That whole incident did not leave me feeling any more confi-dent about the level of brotherhood within the club.

It wasn't too long after that when a guy I knew and trusted from my security days introduced me to a pair of Mounties, and we set up a meeting. They told me they wanted me to inform for them. You know, tell them exactly how the club operated, who was selling dope, that kind of thing. I was surprised that they didn't offer me a big cash reward, just a few hundred bucks here and there. They also pointed out that if I was arrested, they would not acknowledge any relation-ship with me, meaning that I was totally on my own. If the club found out I was telling the feds what they were up to, there would be nobody to come to my rescue. It was essentially a death sentence.

It wasn't much of an offer, but I decided to explore it further anyway, in large part because I was interested to see how these kinds of things worked. So they gave me a test to see how well I could follow instructions. They sent me to a phone booth and instructed me to wait for a call. The caller told me to dial another phone number, and that person would give me further instructions. I was then instructed to get on the Yonge subway line, get out at College

Street, buy a newspaper, get back on the subway headed in the opposite direction, then go eastbound, then westbound, then back downtown to Dundas Street and then Queen Street. I was finally directed to the Royal York Hotel, where they laid out their plan to me in the public dining room. Not a hotel room with a lock and key and some security, but a restaurant where anybody could come and go or sit beside us and listen. In broad daylight, yet. I asked them what our story would be if we happened to run into a club guy. Flustered, they told me they didn't actually have one.

Here was their deal: no acknowledgment, no protection, no real money. I would be a minimum-wage spook. And if I got caught? Well, that was my problem. My first thought? *God, no.* My second thought, after I realized that they didn't know enough not to conduct business in one of the most popular public places in Toronto? *Fuck, no.*

I told Sean and WR what had happened. They could barely believe what they had heard.

I had two or three more meetings with the RCMP contacts, which I'm sure were recorded, but they didn't make a better offer— nor did they inspire any more confidence in me. So eventually I stopped answering their calls and they stopped calling. It just went cold and died.

Things changed, however. I was later approached by two officers from the Ontario Provincial Police Biker Enforcement Unit, which was running a multijurisdictional task force focused on destabilizing OMGs (outlaw motorcycle gangs, which is what they call 1-percenter clubs), particularly the Hells Angels.

Without a doubt, these guys—we'll call them Bob and Bill—were pros. They knew exactly what they were doing, and exactly who I was. They wanted the Downtown chapter pretty badly and knew they needed a full patch on their side to have a fighting chance. But that didn't mean it was easy. Bill just did not get me at all. Bob did, though, and immediately recognized me as a valuable asset.

We met for a few hours. They asked me a lot of questions to establish that I was who I said I was and that I knew everybody they were interested in and what they were doing. It was obvious stuff, like what happens at church, how many members Downtown had, how many chapters there were in Ontario, who held which ranks and what their duties were. They knew all the answers, of course; they were testing my credibility. I aced their test. Once they were satisfied I was telling the truth, things got a bit more intense. When they started asking me about security measures at the clubhouse, I told them I wouldn't say another thing until they made me a deal.

They suggested I talk with a lawyer. They told me I had the right to get my own—of course, I couldn't use the club lawyers—but they suggested I use this guy who often handles these sorts of things for them. I took their guy, and I'm glad I did. I can't say who he is, because I don't want to endanger any of his other clients, but he clearly knew his stuff. When it comes to people like him, you just let them do their jobs.

The deal they made me was amazing—certainly a far cry from what the two bumbling RCMP officers put on the table. The OPP were putting together a multijurisdictional operation called

Project Develop that would target the Hells Angels and associated clubs in Ontario. They said that they would need me for eighteen months. Over that time, they would place $15,000 per month in trust for me to receive at the project's conclusion, and provide $1,800 per week in cash so that I could continue to live the Hells Angels lifestyle without breaking the law for it. There would be another $1,000 per week for any post-arrest testimony. And, if all went to plan, I would be placed in witness protection at the end of the eighteen months. That was, if I qualified for it.

Unlike most people who agree to be police agents, I wasn't desperate to get out of a long prison sentence. I just wanted to get out of the life and start over again. The club had evolved into something entirely different than what I had signed up for, and it had taken over my life, changing it to something I never wanted. A new identity and a few bucks were just what I needed. So I signed up, even though I knew I'd never see my dad again.

At a subsequent meeting, Bob introduced me to detective Todd Dennis of the Durham police. I remember thinking that if we ever made a movie out of all this, Bruce Willis could be perfect for Bob and Tom Cruise could be Todd.

They were both about my age, but had little else in common. Todd was a meticulous note taker, and he had me go through even the most minute steps of every buy and every conversation in painstaking detail. Bob's job was primarily to provide moral support; he had to keep me from falling to pieces. They all kind of did that from time to time, but it was pretty obvious that Bob had drawn the short straw to get that duty.

They then introduced me to Al Rennie, but I already knew him from Project Shirlea. I was right; he had been Sheila's handler. The first words out of my mouth when he entered the room were "Don't you hate me, Al?"

He laughed and replied, "No, Davey, I never did." Then we discussed Project Shirlea and everything that had gone down.

After that, the four of us went over the ground rules associated with being a police agent. They even gave me a bit of a pep talk. They told me that arrests were not as important as my safety, that they weren't trying to put every Hells Angels behind bars (just the ones deeply involved in trafficking) and that it was their intention for me to come out of this in a better situation than I was in now. Fuck, yeah, I was down with that concept.

I was sworn in as a police agent by the commissionaire of oaths. Because everything I did and said could be used in court, the oath was necessary.

Bob then explained my first assignment. I was to make what they called a "controlled buy." That's how they catch traffickers. The agent or undercover cop first proves that he or she doesn't have any contraband on them, then they make a buy while under some kind of surveillance (usually while wearing a recording device). They have to be very careful not to work too hard to initiate the buy because that can open up a window for the trafficker to claim entrapment. Then they hand over the contraband to be used as evidence.

The first target was Juicy. He was born in Tehran, Iran, as Mehrdad Bahman, but we always called him Mark or Juicy. Back in Iran, he was a pretty big wheel. A decorated soldier from the war with Iraq, he was also a heavyweight wrestler who almost made the Iranian Olympic team. After he came to Canada, Mark became an experienced criminal. As a former combat soldier, he was disciplined and aware of his surroundings, and as a former wrestler, he was strong as an ox and knew how to fight. He had developed an impressive network, and was one of those "whatever you need, I can get it" guys. He was also a prospect with the Downtown chapter.

The cops searched me for drugs, fitted me with a wire, handed me a bunch of cash and told me to go buy from Juicy. It was simple. I asked Juicy what he had and he offered me an ounce of coke. I bought it with the cops' money and left. On the outside, it was no big deal, just another day in our world.

But, on the inside, it was an epiphany—I had begun my new life. I had done it; I was now an official undercover agent with one recorded buy under my belt. At the end of the week, Bob handed me $1,800 in cash. I asked him how I was supposed to submit invoices and expense reports for the money. He laughed and told me all I had to do was stay active in the club by going to parties and runs. "Uhhh, okay," I said, dumbfounded. "Thanks."

Everywhere I went, even to parties in Montreal, I was surrounded by an invisible wall of blue. They would watch my every move, not just to ensure my safety, but also to make sure I was doing everything I promised them I would do. That meant I had to keep up the appearances not only of a full-patch Hells Angel, but also of Downtown's sergeant-at-arms.

I was required to speak with my handlers every day, and they would frequently ask me questions about members and prospects—the cops called them all "targets." Bahman, Robin Moulton, Shane, Big Head, Shaun Robinson and Doug Myles were frequent targets. Providing the cops with personal information on the other Hells Angels bothered me, because I was not informed of that part of the job when I signed on. It was frustrating, but I realized I was in too deep to quit.

One day, I was meeting with my handlers at a safe house when they brought in a psychiatrist to chat with me. He was on their payroll, kind of a company shrink. I didn't know why they did that, still don't for sure, but it went all right. It was actually an enjoyable chat. The shrink told me there was no pass or fail, that I should just think of it as two guys talking. So I did. Over lunch, he and I spoke about a lot of things, and we laughed over some of life's great ironies. I guess they wanted to see how I was coping under the pressure.

13

UNDERCOVER

Being an agent means you are totally undercover. It's kind of like you're acting in a movie, except it's not a movie, it's real life. Nobody wrote the story, you have no lines to remember, nobody yells, "Cut!" if things get out of hand, and there are definitely no second chances. When you're undercover, you have to be absolutely perfect for every second of every performance, because the penalty for fucking up is not a bad review—it's your life.

And being undercover, acting quickly became my new way of life. Every morning, I was encouraged to touch base with my handlers so we could set up a meeting at a safe house. It was always the same. I would arrive low-profile—no colors, no jewelry, none of the loud paraphernalia that bikers tend to wear to advertise who they are. And I would never take a direct route. Using the very same methods I had used to shake the cops, I would double back and take indirect routes. I did everything I could to appear nonchalant, so that if I ran into a biker, I could say I was shaking a tail.

When I got there, my handlers and I would go over every detail of my activities since our last meeting. As we went deeper and deeper into the project, the gaps between our meetings would become shorter and shorter.

In order to be paid my $1,800 weekly stipend, I would have to swear to a commissioner of oaths and then go over the same discussion I had already had with my handlers, although I was careful to use more formal and less offensive language.

Then I would be briefed on the identity of my next target. I would never choose my targets, and even to this day, I have no idea how they were picked. But it was clear they knew something, because they had a lot of the heavy hitters in their sights. Of course there was Juicy, along with Mark Bodenstein, Ian Watson, Doug Myles, Shaun Robinson, Lorne Campbell, Robin Moulton, Shane, the two Tommies and Dave Blackwood.

After the takedown, I saw lots of other names (some I didn't recognize), but I knew that they were just associates of the people on my list. Most people have no idea exactly how complicated the dope industry is and how many people it involves. Of course, the stuff has to come from somewhere and has to be stored somewhere. And nobody wants to be caught holding it, or even to be the guy who gave it to the guy who gets caught. So there are always plenty of people involved in every transaction, and each one of them gets a cut.

Of all the targets, Bodenstein was by far the most difficult to get a buy from. He was paranoid to the point of delusion. To get any coke from him, you'd have to jump through a number of hoops that changed all the time, even if he knew you well. Even a simple buy from him was like a trip to the dentist—tedious and painful.

My handlers, however, were very interested in him and told me to hit him up for a key. That's because, as careful as he was about who he sold to, he was a lot less careful about letting his mouth run. In fact, he would tell anyone who'd listen he had the best, purest coke in the city at the lowest prices. Saying you sell coke is not a crime, but actually selling it is. So Bodenstein could advertise all he wanted, as long as he was super careful about who he actually sold to. It was a surprisingly effective way of keeping himself safe from getting charged.

The timing could not have been better. With TC out of the picture in jail, the coke market quickly became very competitive. Bodenstein had heard that I was buying from Juicy, so he wanted in on some of the action.

He approached me at a party, and I asked him if we could talk business later that week. I told him I was interested in buying, but only if the product was up to snuff. He told me he always kept a few packages around, so it would be no problem for me to find out for myself if it was any good or not.

I really believed him and thought there would be no problem. But later in the week, we met up and he didn't have anything on him. He kept making appointments for me to meet him at restaurants around the GTA, and each time, he'd be acting super paranoid and he would not have any samples, let alone any product. Finally, we were at a steakhouse when he followed me into the men's room. I was actually taking a leak when he patted me down for a wire.

When we went back to our table, there was a party of five or six guys in suits seated at the other end of the patio. Even though they hadn't paid any attention to us, Bodenstein walked over, said something to them and gave one of them a thick roll of bills. He came back to our table and told me they were cops, and that they were in his pocket and on his payroll. I never found out if that was true or not. But, more important to me, he still didn't have the stuff.

A couple of nights later, Bodenstein told me to meet him at the Octagon Steakhouse on Yonge Street, up in Thornhill. It was a fancy place, all wood and leather inside. Of course, he wasn't there. I decided to wait for him—he was notorious for being late—by sipping virgin Caesars and eating a shrimp cocktail. When he finally showed up, we did the deal and then he couldn't have gotten the hell out of there fast enough. I mean, I don't like spending more time than is necessary with the guy, but he could have at least had a beer just to keep up appearances. I was getting tired of staying sober anyway.

My handlers were not in the habit of sharing information on our targets, but we all enjoyed a laugh over Bodenstein's extreme measures to shake tails and weed out informants. Funny thing was that it was all ultimately unsuccessful—he was being watched and recorded every second from the time he pulled up to the Octagon to the time he left.

The next target was a lot easier, and one I'm sure the cops were happy to hear more about. His name was Ian Watson, a member from Sudbury. He had a habit of antagonizing police as much as he could. One of the things he did was to take pictures of cops, including undercover ones, and post them in magazines and on websites with a "know your local cops" banner. It wasn't something the club supported. Our general attitude was that it was like poking a stick at an angry dog behind a fence. It's a bad idea because you never know when you might run into that dog without a fence between the two of you. After it all went down, he was charged with threatening a justice official. He wasn't even smart enough to disguise his actions. The threatening charge was later stayed, but lots of guys cited his big mouth as the reason they weren't given bail.

Watson was always up in everybody's business, but was usually pretty laid-back and trusting, so it was easy to get some hash and coke from him. As was his usual way of doing business, his girlfriend, Marisa, did the running and drop-offs for him. I could tell that it gave her kind of a thrill to do that sort of thing. It was her walk on the wild side, while for him it was a way of reducing risk to himself.

After him, the cops told me to go after Shaun Robinson of Oshawa. He was an ex–Satan's Choice member and had a success-ful civilian job as a boilermaker. I once made the mistake of calling him an ironworker and got a long and boring earful of all the differ-ences between the two.

Shaun was a bit difficult for me to deal with. I'm not sure about all the details, but I know that he had been dealing with another Downtown member named Phil Johnson. Somehow, the deal went bad enough for Phil to lose his patch over it. From what I heard, that experience made Shaun reluctant to deal with Downtown guys. So the best way I knew to get to him was through Lorne Campbell, another former member of Satan's Choice who had since become a full-patch Hells Angel with Oshawa.

Lorne and I were becoming friends, as were our girlfriends. I had some reluctance about getting Lorne involved, not just because we were friends, but because I didn't think that he was actually a big-time drug dealer. Morally, I had little problem telling my handlers exactly what full-time criminals like Juicy and Watson were up to, but it was different with Lorne. I knew he used drugs, but I just did not get the impression he was all that big into dealing.

If I had brought such concerns to my handlers, they would quickly have told me that they couldn't explain everything about everyone involved and that if the people involved weren't doing anything wrong, they wouldn't face any charges. Basically, it would have been a polite way of telling me to shut the fuck up and do my job. Not very reassuring.

So Lorne spoke to Shaun on my behalf. I was surprised to learn from him that Shaun was more than willing to deal with me directly because of my strong reputation, even though I was a Downtown guy. That was good, because it allowed me to buy from Shaun without involving Lorne.

Finally, they wanted me to target Doug Myles. I had known Doug longer than anyone else in the club, even longer than my sponsors. We went all the way back to when I was a doorman at the Falcon's Nest. Most everybody I had met since then also knew Doug, and we shared several mutual civilian friends as well. Doug and I did not always see eye to eye, but we were undeniably close.

Besides, he was a drug dealer and I wanted to buy some drugs, so it should be easy, right? Wrong. Doug was a veteran drug dealer, and you don't get to be one of those by taking unnecessary chances.

Doug's whiskers began to twitch when he noticed I had been buying a lot of coke from Juicy. To him, that didn't make much sense. Although it was clear I needed money after Operation Shirlea put us all in jail and TC out of business, what would I be doing with keys of coke? Had I set up my own operation? Before that, all I had done was transport coke. Now, it appeared, I was actually selling it—a far more serious offense in the eyes of the law. Besides, I had never bought any significant quantity of drugs from him before, so why would I need some now, especially since he knew I was getting plenty from Juicy? It was all possible in theory, but just didn't pass the old sniff test.

Doug didn't like it. We might have been friends for years, but a smart drug dealer like Doug doesn't trust anyone, even his closest friends. So when my handlers directed me to buy a key from him, he acted innocent, as though he had never heard the word *cocaine* in his life. "I don't do that," he said when I asked him for coke. "I don't know what you're talking about."

I took that as an indicator that the project I was working on had to end soon. If Doug, who had known me for decades and been through all kinds of shit with me, didn't trust me enough to talk about cocaine in front of me any longer, the club must have known something was going down and that I had to be No. 1 on the list of suspects.

Just as much as they didn't want the cops to know what they were doing, I didn't want them to know what I was doing. But the big difference was what would happen to me if they ever found out. If they even had an inkling that I was on the other side, my life would not be worth much.

Doug might not have trusted me, but he had to keep his business running, so when Dave Blackwood approached him for a key, he was quick to produce one. He just didn't know that Dave was buying it for me (or, to be more precise, the police). In fact, Dave had said in church that he was looking for some investors so that he could buy more coke. I told him that I knew some people who were interested, and that I could talk to them. I just didn't tell him that they were my handlers.

It wasn't easy dealing with Blackwood, either. He had a civilian job and a girlfriend who he wanted to keep out of the life as much as possible. But we managed to arrange a price, a time and a place, so I took off to the safe house and let my handlers know what was going on. A few back-and-forth calls with Blackwood while he was at work let them know this was a real deal.

I arranged to meet Dave at the garage behind where he lived. He had made it into the kind of man cave you might expect, with a cold beer fridge, some girlie calendars and a lot of club paraphernalia. It was pretty sweet, in my opinion. So sweet, I noticed, that it had a pretty sophisticated alarm system.

Just as I was collecting money from my handlers to execute the deal, one of them received a phone call calling it off. Apparently, somebody back at headquarters had his nose out of joint because he hadn't received a memo and hadn't signed off. There was no arguing with him. It was off.

That really threw a monkey wrench into our plans. I mean, it's always bad to back out of any deal, but it was also really unfortunate timing. Unbeknownst to me, two weeks earlier, Blackwood had ordered some coke from Doug Myles, but the deal had fallen through because Blackwood couldn't come up with the cash. Now, Doug was normally a very patient man, but nobody in the drug-dealing business wants to look like a doormat, and his ability to trust Blackwood had been seriously compromised.

Of course, that put a lot of pressure on Blackwood, so when I couldn't come up with the money for the coke I had ordered, he wasn't exactly understanding. We were friends, but he really didn't want to fuck up another deal with Doug. I had to think quickly and dig deep into my repertoire of dance moves. Of course, the whole time, my mind was running with telling him about the OPP officer who obviously had a stick up his ass, but that was not realistically on the table. All I could do was to ask to reschedule for a week later, and hope that the OPP guy would get over it and sign the papers so that we could get on with the deal.

Eventually, the deal did go through. I still remember watching Blackwood walk up to Doug's house with all the money stuffed into the pockets of his cargo pants. You could see the outlines of the little bricks of cash through the canvas and see stray bills sticking out of every pocket.

The ironic part is that it was, as I recall, some pretty shitty coke.

My targets were not just limited to club members. The two Tommies were just as bad as Bodenstein when it came to being paranoid, but they were a lot sloppier. I remember one time when one of the Tommies agreed to make a deal in a Pickering hotel room. When I first got there, I made the room look like I'd been there for a while, as though I had been using it as a home base. Tommy

Christodoulo walked in, made the deal, refused to stay for a beer, took a small sample of coke for his driver and fucked off as quickly as he could. None of his safety precautions prevented him from being recorded, though.

The next guy in my sights was Robin "The Bird" Moulton. He was something else, a real go-getter. When he was a prospect—sponsored by Mark Staples—he actually set up a support store in his hometown of Saint John, New Brunswick, to sell Hells Angels–related gear to people back east. While that was pretty clever in and of itself, the truly impressive part was that he also shipped a little cocaine with every package of support gear. Since it was domestic shipping and didn't cross any borders, the authorities didn't bother to check it. I have to admit, it was a pretty clever plan.

But the boy genius had a big problem. The people he was selling to in the Maritimes had been Juicy's customers, and when he found out, he didn't like that the Bird was horning in on his territory. So Juicy told Mark Staples what was going on. It's traditional that if someone has a problem with a prospect, he would go to the guy's sponsor to mediate.

The Bird, desperate to hold on to his revenue stream, made a huge mistake. He told them it was not actually his coke, but mine, and he went on to tell them that I'd said I would be going down east and sorting everything out. Juicy, who was right to be incredulous, told me Moulton's story, and I realized we all had a major problem on our hands.

I told my handlers, and I also conducted my own investigation. While Staples was quick to come to the defense of his up-and-coming protégé Bird, I tracked down one of the guys down east he was dealing with. Dean Huggan had been with a club called the Four Runners before becoming a full-patch member of Bacchus. The Bacchus MC had gotten pretty big out east after the Hells Angels chapter in Halifax folded, and later even expanded into Ontario. Although they had failed in their bid to become Hell Angels chapters, we still worked and partied with them a lot. They were more autonomous than a support crew, but were definitely our allies.

Huggan told me that when Moulton was in New Brunswick, he dropped my name several times and even threatened to sic the Downtown Toronto sergeant-at-arms (me) on anyone who did not pay in full and on time. That, of course, was news to me.

The situation had gone from serious to dire. It's a major breach of club policy to use the club's name or wear your colors while committing a crime, let alone use another member as a threat. You don't use the club, because it incriminates the club. Of course, it depends on who you are, though. Steve Lindsey and Ray Bonner were convicted of extortion while wearing their club jackets and rings. But they were big-time guys, so nothing much happened to them. On the opposite end of the scale was a guy from Downtown named Roy, who was caught shoplifting a small amount of meat from a grocery store. Personally, I can't think of anything more humiliating than being caught by some untrained, flopdick of a minimum-wage store security guard while wearing your club jacket. I guess I'm lucky, because I had never had to steal anything. But if I had, I'd have used some common sense about it. Soon thereafter, Roy was tossed from the club. I think there was something else going on, because I had seen full patches busted down to prospects or hangarounds for much more serious offenses.

We managed to work it all out internally, though, and nobody paid any major penalty. I probably would have done something more serious about it if I were not desperate to make buys for my handlers and to stay out of trouble. Maybe two weeks later, I managed to get two keys from Moulton, who was working by then with Shaun and another guy who I later heard became an agent whose work resulted in more arrests later on.

14

THE DANGER ZONE

Drugs are one thing, but guns are something else entirely. Whatever your opinion of the War on Drugs might be, you have to realize that when people want something that badly, someone is going to get it to them. And when the thing that you want is illegal, the game changes. People will pay anything, even risk their lives for drugs. The drug trade is all about easy money. People sell fake shit, impure shit, misrepresented shit. They steal from each other, and they jealously guard what they already have. The competition for turf and for customers becomes so great that tempers flare and violence happens. It might be fists, it might be crowbars, it might even be guns.

Hell, we saw that when the Hells Angels and Rock Machine were fighting for the right to sell drugs in Quebec. Both sides set firebombs all over the city, killing each other and innocent civilians. And when some guy shot up a block of bars in downtown St. John's,

Newfoundland, with an AK-47, everybody knew that the Hells Angels and their cocaine were in town.

And that's when my handlers told me to get a gun.

We decided to hit up Juicy because he told me he could acquire anything for me at any time—he was like a one-man crime wave. Besides, he had told me he had several of his own guns to protect himself from other criminals.

That's not uncommon. You can't become a big-time drug dealer without stepping on some toes. And, of course, those toes almost always belong to someone who has no intention of letting you push them out of the way. Because of that, most players in the trafficking business carry a gun, so it was not at all out of character for me to ask Juicy for something small and easy to conceal.

A lot of Hells Angels in Canada have guns, but none of them are legal. Because of some court rulings, no Hells Angel can acquire a fire-arms acquisition certificate, no existing ones are renewed and anyone holding one loses it if they patch over or join the club. I know some guys are upset about it because they grew up hunting and consider them-selves to be responsible firearm owners who store and transport and use their guns in an entirely safe manner. But they'll just have to learn to fish or take pictures, because I don't see the law changing any time soon.

Still, the world Hells Angels live in means many of them feel they need to own guns, so when I asked Juicy for one, he didn't raise an eyebrow. Within a couple of hours, he let me know he had something suitable for me.

Of course, he wanted it out of his hands as quickly as possible, so I had to act fast. I drove to the safe house to tell my handlers it was going down and took some money from them. Then I went to Juicy's house.

There was a young hardcore-looking guy there who handed me a sock with the pistol inside. He told me it came with a few "teeth"—slang for bullets. I paid him the agreed-upon price. I would later learn the sock was to prevent any prints or DNA from getting on the gun. In fact, they showed me how to load it and squeeze the trigger entirely within the sock. All you have to do is drop it at the scene of the crime, and there's nothing but eyewitness testimony to link it back to you. And if there are no witnesses, you're basically safe from prosecution. Even I have to admit it's a pretty brilliant solution to an age-old problem.

Oddly, it wasn't the only gun I was offered that week. I was just hanging out with some friends when some non-member barfly named Darrin started shooting his mouth off about being able to get a gun. I let him know I was interested with the look on my face, but didn't say anything to him directly.

I went to my handlers and told them what had happened. Of course they wanted to take another gun off the streets, but something appeared fishy to them. They didn't trust the idea that some street kid would be openly bragging about being able to get his hands on a gun. In fact, they figured that he was most likely working for the Mounties. After all, the RCMP didn't know I was working for the OPP, and the OPP didn't know who was working for the RCMP.

But I knew that all kinds of criminals like to show off for Hells Angels. It was not uncommon for this sort of thing to happen because, in our world, it makes sense to be on our side. So I convinced the handlers to front me the money.

I made arrangements to meet the guy in a strip mall parking lot in Scarborough. The exchange went smoothly, even though he didn't know the sock trick, and I took the gun back to the safe house.

It was a strange-looking gun, kind of like a Luger from the Second World War. One of my handlers, Craig Pulfrey, was a fire-arms expert, and he couldn't even figure out what caliber it was. But Mike Press from the Guns and Gangs Task Force eventually tested it and got it to work. There's a big difference under the law between selling a gun that works and one that doesn't.

I later bumped into Darrin at a party and he gave me a whole whack of bullets for free. I wasn't supposed to accept the bullets because I was not technically allowed to receive any contraband my handlers didn't know about. But the handlers don't know what it's like to be a Hells Angel. People come up to you all the time and offer you things, and you generally take them unless you have a reason not to. It's part of the job. So when a guy who sold me a crazy old vintage gun offered me free bullets—probably some of the very few bullets on Earth that would fit in the damn thing—I absolutely had to take them or it would arouse serious and lingering suspicion that would spread through the whole community.

I was under strict instructions not to conduct deals that my handlers didn't know about, but I really had no choice. Besides securing my own safety by keeping up the appearances of being a Hells Angel, I knew it was important to get those bullets off the streets.

Because of the gun deal, I kind of owed it to Darrin to spend some time with him. That's sort of the unwritten rule when it comes to bikers: If you do a Hells Angel a favor, you get to hang out with him a bit. A lot of those guys think it's their way into the club, but we kind of already know if we want them or not before it gets to that stage.

After a while, I learned that Darrin wasn't really a bad guy, just someone who was trying too hard to be a criminal. As it turns out, the OPP were wrong about him. He wasn't an agent, and he got busted, but the case against him fell apart.

Even before I really knew anything about bikers, I remember seeing Donny Petersen at Gold's Gym on Eglinton Avenue in Scarborough. He used to ride a motorcycle with some other Para-Dice Riders, and he would work out with some very heavy weights. I respected their, and particularly his, dedication to fitness.

Years later, I was partying at a strip joint with some Para-Dice Riders when I noticed Donny again. He didn't seem to fit in with the other guys. While they could get pretty wild, he was quiet and kept to himself. He was also polite and well spoken, even though he would enjoy an off-color joke from time to time. He didn't seem to espouse the virulent racism that was commonplace with bikers, he didn't seem to swear at all, and I never saw him stoned.

When I began to strike for the Para-Dice Riders, Donny knew about as much about me as I knew about him. After I received my patch and made a strong reputation for myself by organizing parties, cleaning up, and representing myself and the club without being a drunken rip-off artist or dope fiend, Donny got to know me.

As national spokesman, Donny traveled a lot, and he would sometimes bring me along. He'd attend officers' meetings all over

Ontario, Montreal, Calgary, and even places like Austria and South Africa. I liked traveling with Donny. He quite accurately referred to himself as a "low-maintenance member" because he never expected anyone to drive him around or get him dope or girls. He'd simply enjoy a few beers after a day of sightseeing squeezed in between painfully boring but mandatory meetings.

On the way, he'd always want to talk about bikes, but I was out of my element there. Sure, I liked to ride, but my knowledge stopped not far after that. When he realized he had plumbed the depths of my motorcycle knowledge, he'd move onto another topic, like his mom and his family.

Of course, once I became an agent, my handlers were quite eager for me to attend those kinds of meetings. And they wanted to make Donny a target. I had some major problems with that. It wasn't that I liked Donny more than the other guys; I just really couldn't think of him as a criminal because I had never seen him break the law. When I voiced my concerns, the OPP brought in one of their most respected staff sergeants to explain the concept of "facilitating crime" to me. When he was done, I still thought it was a gray area at best. I had no problem exposing people who were actually committing crimes, but to get a guy in trouble because he had lots of friends who were criminals did not sit well with my conscience.

So it always seemed like it took a few years off my life whenever I would speak with Donny while I was wearing a wire. He had always said I was a sensitive guy, and I think he was right. I've come to believe that it's the stronger man who expresses his emotions rather than swallowing them and allowing them to fester.

At that time, my feelings were running roughshod. While I was working as an agent, a multijurisdictional task force arrested twenty-seven people, including fifteen Hells Angels, and seized $3 million worth of drugs, primarily cocaine and ecstasy. Among those taken down were Gerald "Skinny" Ward, Stadnick's old friend who ran Niagara.

What bothered me about it was how it happened—or, rather, *who* had made it happen. Stephen Gault, whom I never had much respect for, had become an agent and had taken almost a million dollars to record the goings-on of his brothers. Obviously, I understood the circumstances—he had turned agent and avoided a long jail sentence—but he did it without any discretion or care for his club brothers. Donny was arrested, but got out on bail. Of course, the charges didn't stick.

While I was at church, we talked about Gault, and I was recording the whole thing. Of course, I mentally separated Gault and myself. Yes, we were both police agents, but he was doing it to save his own skin and he was a real hardcore criminal—he had even bragged about killing people. I, on the other hand, was just trying to get out of a life that had spun out of control.

In total, I lasted about fifteen months as an agent. My job was to record myself buying drugs and other contraband, and I certainly did that. Over that period, I made large buys from all kinds of players, members and non-members alike, including Sebastian Mihelovic, Cam Spicer's team, Robin Moulton, Shaun and Lorne, Dave Blackwood, the Tommies, Ian Watson and a few others. One of them was Nick Nero, who later became famous for driving his Ferrari and Maserati while living in a halfway house after he got out. His freedom didn't last long, though. He went down for hiring a hit man to kill John "Johnny Maserati" Raposo on the busy patio of a Toronto coffee restaurant.

It was hard work being an agent, and I did my very best. George Cousens and Craig Pulfrey were okay guys, for cops, and we had a few laughs, but they were never anything less than totally professional. They worked hard, all hours of the day and night, and sacrificed a lot for this project.

The club was getting paranoid. After the Project Shirlea busts, nobody knew who to trust, nobody knew who was listening to what. And it wasn't just the police; we were all watching each other, and then accusations started to emerge. One time, a guy named Ernie told Doug Myles that I had pocketed a big roll of cash when I was sweeping the clubhouse for bugs.

I was enraged. I eventually tracked the guy down—I hunted him everywhere—called him a liar in front of everyone and let him and everyone else know that I had never taken a dime from anyone. Hell, they all knew that of every dime I had, I'd usually give away seven cents of it.

That was the way it was after the mass arrest. You had to prove yourself all the time, because everyone was a suspect.

The life was wearing on a lot of guys, not just me. A perfect example would be Carl. He had a great job as a teamster and really enjoyed himself drinking and riding with the Para-Dice Riders. But after the patch-over, he was immediately out of work and dependent on the club for everything. The same thing was true with Dennis, a guy we called "the Rainman." He had a couple of jobs delivering supplies to constructions sites and driving a tow truck while he was a Para-Dice Rider. He had a great bike and a wonderful girlfriend named Barb. After the patch-over, he was a Hells Angel, but he had lost both his jobs and his girlfriend and always had trouble scraping two nickels together.

The anger, paranoia and stress of being a Hells Angel made me long for the old days before the patch-over. But we were all still friends—at least that's what we told each other. And there was some truth to it. While I was an agent, I did spend some time away from my OPP handlers. Juicy, Dirtbag and Paul the Wop invited me to go to the East Coast for a Bacchus party. They also invited BeBop. He wasn't in the club, but he was everybody's friend. We wanted to ride our bikes, but Hurricane Katrina had other ideas. We knew we would have been washed away if we had tried.

Luckily, the ever-resourceful Juicy knew a travel agent, and she made flight and hotel arrangements for us in less than a minute.

While we were out there, we went fishing. The bunch of us took a boat out and got totally skunked. Not even a nibble. Frustrated, we tried again the next day, but this time we took along a French-Canadian guide. Marcel was hardcore, maybe even a little crazy, but he was an old guy who everyone in the area said knew the river like the back of his hand. He took us out and, all of a sudden, we were bagging walleye like they wanted to be caught.

We were so excited that I thought I'd lighten the mood even further, so I turned to BeBop and asked him if I should mark the spot so we could come back again. He agreed it was a good idea, so I took a Sharpie out of my pocket and put an *X* on the side of the boat.

Marcel looked at me and said in his thick Quebecois accent that it was the stupidest thing he had ever seen anyone do.

BeBop agreed because, he said, we might not use the same boat next time.

Naturally, I felt exposed and in danger the whole time, but it really ramped up after the trip when I went to a church meeting and there was a discussion about a rat in our midst. As the members were angrily discussing what they would do once he was caught and assuring themselves it wouldn't be long before he was exposed, I couldn't help but wonder whether I was there because I wasn't a suspect or because I was.

After I left, I told my handlers what had happened. I was nervous, even though I knew they were closely monitoring the phone calls, texts and emails the members were sending. In fact, it got so bad that I had to stop the car, open my door and throw up on the pavement before I even got home.

The next three days were murder on my system. I was in the middle of a precarious juggling act in which I was trying not to lie to anybody, while still doing my job and doing my best not to expose myself. I don't care what anyone says or thinks, it was more than most people could take. It was eating away at my body and my very soul like a sickness.

I had to have all my stories and secrets straight. If I had bought drugs from one person, and I was talking to another person, I had to intentionally mislead them on what I was doing so as not to arouse undue suspicion or lead them to the other guy. All the while, though, I had to keep them talking and incriminating themselves. The stress was nearly unbearable. I felt like my whole system was going to give out at any time. I had to wear a heart monitor to know if it was all going to blow or not.

But the stresses of being an undercover agent can't be gauged by any monitor. In the morning, I would wake up and quickly assume whichever character I had to be, depending on who was around. I'd quickly change, and then I would usually have to take on a different persona with someone else on the street or in the gym. After that, I'd go and report to my handlers in a safe house, using that persona. I had to do my best to be honest and sincere with them at all times, but it was hard to peel off the skins, all made of networks of lies, that I had developed during the project. After that, I would meet up with friends or take care of club business, wearing yet another mask.

No matter how tough you think you are, that kind of stress takes a toll. The very fabric of your being changes. And there are physical consequences. Not only was my heart running like a Formula 1 engine, but I would sometimes—maybe three or four times—feel a jolt, almost like some unseen person had given me a shake.

While playing completely different characters in front of the club, my OPP handlers, my family and the girls I was seeing, lying became natural. If I told someone I was getting gas at a station on Eglinton, I'd go to one at Warden and Birchmount instead. If I said I was headed to BeBop's, I'd go to Brewer's instead. It was all a big misinformation campaign just to separate myself from the other guys. But they shouldn't have been surprised by that; it's their way of life. I'd seen every member lie to another's face when I was a prospect.

But for me, it was different. I hated lying, and it and the life I was living felt like I was on a perpetual-motion machine fueled by steroids and speed. It just kept getting faster. It wasn't going to stop by itself. Somebody had to pull the plug or it would crash.

I knew the jig was up when I found out that Doug Myles had started hearing rumors about me. My handlers also knew my period as an agent was coming to an end, so they started sending me on Hail Mary missions, trying to buy as much drugs from as many people as possible. They clearly wanted as many fish in their net as they could land before they pulled it up onto their boat.

I didn't know it at the time, but there had been a number of club meetings behind closed doors about me and my activities. Maybe I'd pushed them all too hard, but they definitely knew something was up with me. They elected Doug Myles to confront me about my activities. The meeting was to be at his garage.

I told my handlers that Doug wanted to meet with me, so they hooked me up with a wire. When I got to Doug's house that night, he greeted me, saying, "Hello, young man," and escorted me to his garage. I say garage, but it was really more of a man cave, with a few bikes, a beer fridge, lots of tools and some posters and photos of the good old days.

I shouldn't have to tell you I was nervous. I was on edge all the time when I was an agent, but this was entirely different. It was a one-on-one meeting with Doug, who I knew suspected something was up with me. I kept my back to the door the whole time so that I could have an unobstructed pathway if I had to bolt. But deep inside, I knew that if it all went down, I wouldn't be running anywhere.

The first thing Doug asked me was, "Has anything happened to you in the last six months?"

That was funny, I thought, because I had been an agent for a lot longer than that. I told him no, and asked him what he meant.

"Are you trying to get people arrested?"

I laughed and asked him what he was talking about.

I could see by his face that there was a lot going on in Doug's mind and that he didn't have a good plan on what order to spill it in.

The previous day, I had bought a kilo of cocaine from Nick Nero. He wasn't a biker, but everybody knew him. Doug brought that up and asked me why I needed a kilo from him when I had just bought two kilos a few days earlier. He wanted to know where all that cocaine was going. I told him I had a guy in the Waterloo area—a guy I used to play football with—and then I stopped explaining and asked him why he needed to know.

He just shook his head and said, "It doesn't make sense."

Then he asked me if I had cornered a member named Pierre in the clubhouse and asked him for pot. Pierre was a pot grower and dealer, so it made sense I would get pot from him. I told Doug to give me a fucking break, asked him what he was talking about and told him I had to make a buck somehow. And although the rule is not to do business in the clubhouse, I asked him which one of us didn't do that from time to time.

"You're not allowed to do that," he told me sternly, ignoring the fact that business was done routinely in the clubhouse. "Everybody knows that."

I finally asked him, "What the fuck is this all about?"

He didn't answer my question. Instead, he told me that Bully said I owed him money from the guy who owned the construction-related business in Woodbridge. Bully told Doug that I'd been paid by the Woodbridge guy, but hadn't given Bully his cut. I tried to deny that, but he interrupted me and kept on going. He also told me Henry said I owed him $18,000. I told him that those transactions were between Henry and Billy Dawson—I was just the middleman. If Henry wants his money, I said, he should be talking to Billy. Fuck him, I added.

It was clear that Doug had canvassed the room at those closed-door meetings to see exactly what I had been doing, so I knew it would not be to my advantage to try to play dumb. Instead, standing on my many years of trustworthy service to the club, I chose to let him know I was offended. I asked him why, if there was suspicion in the club, I didn't have a bullet in my head.

"That's why we're here right now."

It was the most sobering sentence I had ever heard. Was I going to die that night? Was Doug the man who would kill me?

I was in a trance until Doug pointed out that we went back a long way and that we had had some great times and fun over the years. I'd been a Hells Angel since they arrived in Ontario in December 2000.

While he was talking, I couldn't help thinking that brothers don't put bullets in their brothers' heads. This whole thing was all about money, and it had been since the patch-over. It's all about getting ahead, and it doesn't matter who gets stepped on in the process. Were the people I considered family seriously considering murdering me over money? It was a chilling thought.

Still, I wasn't dead yet, so I had to mount a defense of some sort. I decided to play indignant, as though I should be above suspicion because of my long and sterling record with the club. Acting enraged, I said that if any of those guys wanted to talk shit about me, they could do it face-to-face. And as far as drug talk in the clubhouse went, since Larry Pooler had given me a Percodan in the clubhouse, I guess there had to be a meeting about him too. "What the fuck are you talking about?" I asked him. "We all break the rules like that all the time."

I don't remember exactly how I left, but I knew that I was plenty pissed off, but also grateful for Doug's loyalty and friendship. I was pretty sure that if it weren't for his intervention, I probably would have had a bullet in my head instead of a calm one-on-one meeting in a garage.

I got in a rental car and I let my handlers know what happened on the way. They said they noticed something different in my voice, like I was upset. What an understatement. I was in the throes of a cosmic shift. I literally felt different about everything in my life, and have ever since. The feeling that I had come very close to being killed by my closest friends made me realize I am ultimately responsible for all of the choices in my life. It had always been easy for me simply to follow the flow of my life, and have it dictated by other people and situations, from the bars, the security companies, the club and now my handlers from the OPP. But then I came to the realization that none of this was their doing; it was all mine.

But my handlers were right. I was different after the meeting. I was jumpy, I had constant tremors in my hands and a ringing in my ears. I was hostile and very quick-tempered. I'm not sure exactly what it was, but I have been told that it's very much like the way people get when they've been kidnapped.

I realized it was time to take an inventory right then and there. I did not know what was going to happen. Maybe I was going to die and maybe I wasn't. But I also knew that I had committed to this path, that it was the right thing to do and that I absolutely had to follow through.

I went home. I started with a few shots of whiskey before moving to vodka, then beer and hash. I just didn't feel safe anymore. The stress was getting to me. I grabbed my phone—I don't even know who I was going to call—and just started squeezing until its face popped off. Then, I guess, I drifted off to sleep.

The next day, I was due to put in a bar shift at the clubhouse. I had no choice but to trust my handlers as I walked calmly into the lion's den without any idea of what was waiting for me. But I did know that I was not free once I walked inside. The clubhouse is designed in such a way that once the doors lock, it's a good twenty minutes to half an hour before anyone can get inside from the outside, even with explosives. I could be dead and disposed of before the cops could get it open. When the door shut behind me, it gave me a feeling of finality that no jail cell door ever could.

To my surprise and relief, my bar shift went without incident. Everyone was putting on their best face, even though we all knew that they had been talking shit about me behind my back and that many of them suspected me of being an agent. It was the Hells Angels way. Even if you want a guy dead, you smile and laugh with him. Maybe we were brothers after all—just not the way I wanted to be.

And that was it. My handlers knew it would be too dangerous to continue, so they pulled me out of the project the following morning. I was removed from my home and put in a safe house along with a bunch of stuff from my apartment. I knew the day was coming soon, so I had most of my stuff already packed and had also taken my things from the clubhouse and my dad's place.

My handlers and my brothers in the club had the same goal: for David Atwell to vanish from the face of the Earth.

For the next week, my only human contact was with my handlers. To keep up appearances, I was allowed to talk on the phone to family members and some girls I had been seeing. I couldn't tell anyone but my dad. I was pretty sure the club members knew exactly what was going on, but they did their best to keep up appearances as well. They called me constantly, leaving kind-sounding voice-mail messages asking me if I was okay and offering to help me. But I had no doubt it was all a ruse and that they couldn't wait to get their hands on me.

About two or three weeks after I disappeared from the streets, my handlers had me call Dave Blackwood. They had given me a script and instructions that I was to stay within certain boundaries and only describe things generically. The message was simply that I wasn't coming back. If I told him I was still part of the club or that I wanted to continue in business, it would raise a lot of unnecessary complications.

The message was intended to start some chatter among the individual members. Those who had something to worry about were immediately calling, texting and emailing away. Others, like Donny, had nothing to hide and went about their business as usual.

Of course, I was in mortal danger if I was caught outside the safe house. That was brought home when Doug Myles took it upon himself to visit my dad. According to my father, he was mowing the front lawn when Doug drove up and started in with some casual banter before asking if he'd seen me recently. My dad said he hadn't, and Doug left without incident. Say what you will about Hells Angels, they do know right from wrong. I knew and liked Doug's parents, and he was cool with my dad. He knew as well as I did that my father was not responsible for my actions, and left him alone and out of the loop.

It was over. I had gone from high school tough guy to security guard to Para-Dice Rider to Hells Angel, and it was all over. I couldn't go back to any of those things. In fact, I wasn't even going to be David Atwell any more. Everything would be new. At least some of the Hells Angels kind of got their wish—Dave Atwell was dead. But that didn't mean he couldn't testify.

15

OUT OF MY HANDS

Witness protection is serious business. The handlers have it tough. They have precious cargo in their hands. If something were to happen to the witness, all of their work would be down the drain and the bad guys would win.

Now imagine how hard it is for the witness. Not only is your life in danger at every moment of the day and night, with you relying entirely on the competency and dedication of your handlers, but you are also entering the realm of the utterly unknown. When they take you, you have no idea what's going to happen to you. You have no idea what your name will be, where you'll live, what you will do for the rest of your life, or who your friends will be. And you also never know if you will be walking down a street one day, bump into the wrong person and have it all end then and there.

The night before the takedown, they let me know it would be going down the next morning. Even though I knew that a lot of the people

I had been close to for years would have their lives changed forever, there was not a lot I could do other than pop a few movies in the VCR (yeah, a VCR—it was not exactly cutting-edge technology). Did I feel guilty? Not really. I went back to the game philosophy. These guys knew what they had signed up for. If you sell drugs or guns, there's a very strong chance that you will get caught if you don't get killed. The fact that I was behind what would happen to them didn't make a huge difference. If it weren't me, it would have been some other guy they hadn't treated right.

My work for the government paid huge dividends. At six in the morning on April 4, 2007, more than five hundred cops from eighteen agencies stormed clubhouses and residences in Ontario, British Columbia and New Brunswick. Before an hour was up, thirty-one people with ties to the Hells Angels and Bacchus were arrested and facing 169 charges. They also took $3 million in drugs, $500,000 in cash and $500,000 in other property, including bikes and cars.

They took the clubhouse on Eastern Avenue. They couldn't blow the door down, so they hooked a tow truck to the wall facing on the building's west side and pulled the bricks out. By noon, they were making a big show in front of the media's cameras of carrying out anything that said "Hells Angels" or had a winged skull on it.

The cops were jubilant. They were telling anyone who would listen that they had shut down the mighty Hells Angels, in particular the powerful Downtown Toronto chapter. "We are here to shut you down," crowed Ontario Provincial Police Commissioner Julian Fantino at the subsequent media conference. "You can run, but you can't hide. And we will do all that we can to bring you to justice." He kind of sounded like a biker.

He was wrong, though. We all—cops and bikers alike, if not the media and the public—knew it was just a bump in the road for the Hells Angels in Toronto. The cocaine would keep flowing. It just might be more scarce and cost more for a little while, but it would come back.

Project Develop was over. Almost everyone I knew was behind bars, and I was locked in a safe house.

My handlers could tell I was a nervous wreck, and Al Rennie told me that the hardest part of the whole thing is the period between the takedown and the testifying. For me, that was close to two years, just sitting and stewing and cooling my heels.

I'd like to detail the transformation process, because it's fascinating, but I promised my handlers that I wouldn't. But I can say that what emerged was an absolute blank slate. They gave me plenty of instructions and advice, but one thing stuck with me: Fuck this up and you're fucked forever, but follow the instructions and it works.

The money sure helped. Some guys in the program don't negotiate any cash settlement, and I have no idea how they do it. My deal gave me $450,000, plus what was left of my weekly payments, plus $1,000 a week while I was testifying.

It's impossible to start a new life with one foot still in your old one, so I had to cut all ties with everyone I had known before, including my dad, all my friends, the girls I had been seeing, everybody. I couldn't take any courses or get a job because it would be impossible for me to explain why I had to be flown away to court for weeks on end.

So instead, all I could do was to try to do my best to blend into my new city, and go about my business as inconspicuously as possible. I had always taken pride in being the guy people noticed, and now I had to be exactly the opposite. There was not a lot for me to do but watch a lot of movies and reflect on my life, hoping that I could find some kind of personal growth in all of it. My big take-away was that you lace up your skates, you put on your helmet and you get on the ice knowing all the rules. If you get blindsided, that's just part of it; if your teammate doesn't pass to you and takes the shot himself, that's the game, and if you lose 4–0, that's the game too. You just go out there and do your best with what you've got.

I know it's a cliché, but I kept going back to what Robin Moulton always used to say: "Don't hate the player, hate the game." It's something of a throwaway line to most people, but when you've been through something like I've been, it gains a much deeper meaning.

While I did everything I could to put it all into perspective, the stress was overwhelming at times. Because it was affecting my overall health, especially my heart, I was given a prescription for stress-reducing meds. I was literally worried sick, and it was breaking my heart.

I remember being told repeatedly when I became a biker that I would lose my job, I'd lose my girl and I'd go to jail. It all came true, but I had also lost my friends, my family and my very identity.

Plenty of people have said I was being selfish by taking the government's money and a new identity, but if you knew what I went through as an agent, while testifying, and even in my post-biker life without family or friends, you would know that I didn't really gain anything. In fact, I considered what I was doing to be altruistic in a way. Perhaps I'm rationalizing, but I like to think I did something good in getting drugs and guns off the streets and disrupting the Hells Angels' criminal empire, even if it was just for a small time and in a small way.

Just like the guys I was to testify against, my freedom of movement was severely restricted. I was, in effect, under lockdown. I couldn't cook my own meals, let alone go outside for one. The accommodations weren't exactly the Taj Mahal; in fact, it was very basic, almost like basic training in the army. The biggest difference was that the guys behind bars could talk to each other, the other inmates and even the guards. Not me. If one of my handlers was caught shooting the shit with me about a hockey game or anything else, they would be out of there in a matter of minutes. They were polite and courteous, of course, truly professional, but not much in the way of company. But even if they weren't under orders to keep their distance, it's not like they would be my friends. Witness protection is like any other job. These guys had their own friends and family to get back to when quitting time rolled round, and I could always tell they were looking forward to that. I don't blame them, but it was hard for me to know that they punched out at a certain time, while this was my life now. I have to give them credit; they treated me right and it's a very tough job—nobody stays in it for very long.

Every day before I was set to appear in court, I would receive a laptop and a whole bunch of evidentiary disclosure containing audio recordings that had been transcribed into written notes. I would read them and try to make heads or tails out of them. Sometimes it was hard to bring my memory back to certain events because the latest of them was more than two years old, and the oldest was more like five.

Of all the guys arrested, some were released and the smart ones pleaded out. BeBop didn't get in any trouble. Neither did Hoyle or, of course, Petersen. The ones who bargained down to lesser charges did some brief time or were released with stips. In fact, most of those guys finished their sentences—stipulations and all—and were back with the club before the others even had a chance to show up in court.

Because of my situation, I testified under heavy guard when I went to court. Even as a personal protection expert, I was in awe of how sophisticated they were. My old boss, WR, once told me that any good security system has to disrupt your life a little—well, mine could hardly have been disrupted more.

The cops were not only aware of where any potential targets were, but they kept close eyes on the accused and any associates they might have communicated with recently.

And it was no small feat. With trials as big and as hyped as the ones I was involved with, hundreds of people show up to see the proceedings for themselves, and most of them are definitely, even viscerally, on the side of the accused.

After I was sworn in for the first time, I sat down and looked at all of the accused. My eyes immediately went to the Tommies because they were glaring at me. It was obvious how pissed they were, and the look they gave me was nothing short of homicidal. I remember thinking to myself how stupid that was, because if *I* could see them, so could the judge. And to try to intimidate a witness, even if it is just with a glare, seems to me like telegraphing your guilt.

I guess their lawyers did not prepare them as well as mine had me. The Crown's philosophy was that the truth gets them every time. They told me to stick to the truth and to never embellish. I was instructed to take a few seconds to think after I was asked a question, and never to panic. My answers, they said, should only reflect exactly what was asked and that I should never try to interpret what the lawyer was getting at or predict what the next question would be. And, most important, I should not worry about sticking to a script or trying to please the judge, jury or anyone else. All that mattered was the truth, not my opinion of it.

At the mega-trial, I counted twenty-one lawyers against me, all being paid by legal aid or wealthy "well-wishers" or "friends of the club," all doing their best to stare me down and intimidate me. It was, to me, 21–1. I didn't count the Crown attorneys as being on my side because they are bound by the protocols of the court. They couldn't help me; I was up against the defense attorneys alone. My only weapon was the truth.

That's not how defense attorneys see it. To them, it's a game. It doesn't matter if their client is guilty as fuck. It's their job to use any little trick they can find or devise to get him off—the truth be damned. A lot of it is just for show, George Cousens assured me. That way, they're seen as earning their paycheck and will get more work in the future. To them, it's a contest. It's not about guilty or innocent, it's about who wins. Part of their strategy with me emerged pretty quickly. They came at me hard right from the start. I guessed they thought they could hurt my pride enough for me to lose my cool. They were wrong. I got so frustrated with them that I wouldn't even speak directly to them, instead replying directly to the judge, but they never managed to get me to slip up.

The cast of defense attorneys the Hells Angels collected featured some real characters. The first guy I noticed was Anthony Bryant—the guy who defended Paul Bernardo.

Another guy who stood out is Glenn Orr. I can't really say anything bad about Glenn. He certainly does his best. He's what we called a club lawyer. He's made a big part of his career representing Hells Angels in court.

Things took a turn for the ridiculous when Larry Pooler—hardly the most eloquent of our little group—decided to represent himself. Much to my surprise, the trial did not immediately devolve into a circus. In fact, the judge gave him a startling amount of leeway, and the media began to support his efforts. They were treating him like Robin Hood, rather than just another drug dealer. But I certainly don't remember him giving anything to the poor.

In the end, I kind of feel happy for Larry. Even though he broke a cardinal club rule—do not sell drugs in the clubhouse—he kept his patch. In fact, because he was guilty of selling in the clubhouse, the government was able to seize it, costing the club at least $700,000 for the property alone. Of course, a faux pas like that would normally cost anyone his patch, so, if the club still works the way it did when I was with them, I'd bet he had some kind of backdoor deal with someone—and several someones—to keep it. And I also have a feeling that, once the power structure changes, even just a little bit, he'll be out on his ass.

Although my part in the trials did not take that long, I've been told that some of the cases dragged on for seven years. For the most part, Operation Develop was successful, as lots of Hells Angels were convicted. But once again, the club managed to survive. The courts could call the Hells Angels a criminal organization, but they couldn't shut it down.

When it all came to pass, most of the guys convicted were released for time served. Most of them went right back to the club the second they could, but there were some exceptions. Since the trials, I've heard that Lorne Campbell quit because he was so disgusted with the way the club handled things for him when he was in jail and the way the other Hells Angels behaved behind bars. It turned him off the club, and he wanted no part of it after that. Doug Myles quit, and I'm pretty sure it was because of the decision he had had to make about me. Juicy quit, and so did Ian Watson.

The club is still there, operating without an official clubhouse and with a lot of new members. They did open a retail store on Carlaw Avenue, not far from where the old clubhouse was. The Ontario government held on to the clubhouse for a while, and sold it to an undisclosed bidder for an undisclosed price in January 2016. From what I hear, the new owner plans to tear down what the *Globe and Mail* called "an inelegant cinderblock establishment" and put up yet another luxury condo. "Nobody wants a bunker that's just empty and derelict," said Toronto Ward 30 Councillor Paula Fletcher after the announcement. I guess she's right.

For me now, my days are filled with building a new life little by little. I don't see my family or my old friends. Even my handlers are gone, having moved on to new projects. It was a huge shock, actually, when it all ended. Before the takedown, my days were filled with club activities, meeting with my handlers and setting up buys. Afterward, it was kind of boring. I had to study the transcripts, prepare my testimony and appear in court. But after my part of the trial was over, there was nothing. All the necessary activities in my life came to a screeching halt. There was hour after hour of nothing to do but think. I was totally alone, without a friend in the world. Dave Atwell was dead, but I kept going.

It's hard to explain, but the situation reminded me of one time in the 1980s when I was working security. I was bored and wanted a coffee, so I drove out of the neighborhood, through Forest Hill to Rosedale. Not much later, I found myself at a Country Style doughnut shop on Davenport Road. Instead of rolling back to Forest Hill afterward, I drove over to the corner of Yonge and Bloor, stopped the car and got out. It was maybe four in the morning, and when I looked up to the sky over the buildings, I could see that the sun would be rising soon. In a few hours, this very spot, this intersection—the busiest in all of Canada—would be teeming with people and cars and life. But, at that moment, it was just me, all alone in near silence. That's kind of how it was for me after the trial. I was aware—through memories and my own projections—of all the people and the action around me, but I just wasn't part of it anymore.

Adjusting to life after years in the club is more difficult than you might expect. When you're a Hells Angel, people know right away and treat you accordingly. They might respect you, envy you or even hate you, but they don't—*can't*—ignore you. But after I left, I was no longer defined by the patch. When I was a Hells Angel, people (especially civilians) would tread lightly around me; they'd respect my space.

But now, every bonehead does whatever bullshit he feels like. I'm a pretty big guy who's very handy in a fight, but I can't just haul off and punch some guy in the face—no matter how much he deserves it—without him screaming to the cops. People don't move out of my way now, I don't get anything for free anymore and I have to meet and pursue women just like any other guy.

That's my life now. Just a regular Joe. A nobody.

ACKNOWLEDGMENTS

I'd like to thank my friends and my family for their understanding. It's all about doing what's right.

—Dave Atwell

My contribution to *The Hard Way Out* could not have happened had it not been for Dave's courage in reaching out to make sure his story was told. It would also not have been possible without the help of Len Isnor, formerly of the Ontario Provincial Police, who helped bring the two of us together. *The Hard Way Out* was also made possible by a number of sources inside and outside of law enforcement and Canadian motorcycle-club culture who corroborated the history behind the book.

The book happened because of the good people at Harper-Collins Canada, in particular Jim Gifford, Maria Golikova, Natalie Meditsky, Melissa Nowakowski and Jeremy Rawlings.

And, of course, I have to thank my wife and sons for putting up with me, and thanks, as always, to Leta Potter.

—Jerry Langton